AMERICAN SIGN LANGUAGE WORKBOOK

AMERICAN SIGN LANGUAGE WORKBOOK

EXERCISES TO BUILD YOUR SIGNING VOCABULARY

Rochelle Barlow

PHOTOGRAPHY BY **James Bueti**

ROCKRIDGE PRESS

Benjamin, Jenée, Jackson, Madison, Spencer, and Lincoln. Every day I get to be your mother is the best day. My heart overflows with delight, love, and gratitude.

For general information on our other products and services or to obtain technical support, please contact our Customer Care Department within the United States at (866) 744-2665, or outside the United States at (510) 253-0500.

Rockridge Press publishes its books in a variety of electronic and print formats. Some content that appears in print may not be available in electronic books, and vice versa.

TRADEMARKS: Rockridge Press and the Rockridge Press logo are trademarks or registered trademarks of Callisto Media Inc. and/or its affiliates, in the United States and other countries, and may not be used without written permission. All other trademarks are the property of their respective owners. Rockridge Press is not associated with any product or vendor mentioned in this book.

Interior and Cover Designer: Emma Hall
Art Producer: Meg Baggott
Editor: Erin Nelson
Production Editor: Nora Milman

Photography © 2020 James Bueti. Styling by Bethany Eskandani.

ISBN: Print 978-1-64611-950-9
eBook 978-1-64611-951-6

R0

CONTENTS

INTRODUCTION

I developed an interest in sign language when, decades ago, my grandmama first read *Koko's Kitten* to me. It was a story about a gorilla that learned sign language to communicate with humans. Such communication turned into an unspoken bond between Koko and his series of cat friends. The combination of my obsession with gorillas and the power of this unique language to connect living beings was irresistible to me. I was quite reserved and shy; I rarely spoke, and when I did, I mumbled due to extreme discomfort and anxiety.

My mother, an insightful person, fueled my passion with dictionaries, books, and learning opportunities. My initial reasons for learning quickly turned into passion for the language and a deep desire to communicate within the Deaf community.

My path to where I am today has been full of adventure and sprinkled with ups and downs. I began interpreting at the age of 17—a terrifying learn-as-you-go situation that I credit for a significant portion of my growth. During and after college, I tutored, volunteered, and continued to interpret for classes and extracurricular functions. Altogether, I've interpreted for over 15 years, mainly in the higher education system. When I had my own children, I began teaching individuals and families, and seven years ago, I moved teaching to my website to help more people looking for affordable ASL instruction.

My time learning ASL was not all easy and enjoyable, and there were times when I wanted to give up. I was sometimes frustrated with the lack of resources, clear instruction, and intuitive steps to reach fluency. If you've found yourself frustrated or not sure where to start, I can relate. I suspect that your ASL learning journey will be like mine in some ways but ultimately your own.

You may be losing your hearing and need to learn ASL because your ability to communicate with your family and friends is deteriorating. You need help, you need to learn it right away, and the process needs to be easy. You need a way to encourage your family and friends to learn it with you without them being overwhelmed.

My mission in the ASL world is to make learning sign language straightforward, simple, and fun. I'm tired of seeing so many ASL learners like yourself scramble to find a reliable resource to get you from not knowing any ASL to meaningfully signing with others. (And fast!) If you're looking for a simple and effective resource to learn signs, build sentences, and check your retention—you've come to the right place.

Here you'll find easy-to-follow images, practical exercises, accurate and up-to-date information, and instructions on how to put the signs together to build sentences. This workbook is also an easy way to get your family on board and learning ASL alongside you. As you begin your journey, know that with each lesson you are one step closer to ASL communication. Most importantly, remember that you are not alone.

WHAT IS ASL?

ASL is a visual language based on specific hand gestures and their placement relative to the body along with head and body movements, mouth morphemes (the specific movements you make with your mouth to add meaning to a sign), facial expressions, and other non-manual markers. You express ASL with your hands, body, and face. You receive it with your eyes.

The grammar for sign language is structured quite differently from English grammar. It is a robust, expressive, and evolving language with as much information expressed as any oral language.

It's important to know that American Sign Language is not a universal sign language. It is only used in the United States and Canada. As you explore North America, you'll find regional signs, or dialects, just as you would hear various accents and slang across the same regions.

A Brief History

American Sign Language's history is long, and its journey to existence is rocky. Since the time of Aristotle, the Deaf were considered non-persons and were treated as such until the Renaissance. In the 1700s, Charles-Michel de l'Épée, known as the Father of the Deaf, aimed to right this prejudice, creating an educational method for sign language. This made signing available to the public and educators. De l'Épée's methods went on to inspire Laurent Clerc, a French Deaf teacher.

In 1815, Clerc met Thomas Hopkins Gallaudet, an American also searching for a way to educate the Deaf. Gallaudet invited Clerc to come to the United States, where Gallaudet taught Clerc English and Clerc taught Gallaudet sign language. Together they established the first school for the Deaf in Hartford, Connecticut, where it still stands today. Americans have used ASL since then, but language experts did not recognize it as a true language until 1960.

Who Is This Book For?

This workbook is for the person who always wanted to learn American Sign Language. It's for the person who is losing their hearing or knows someone who is. It's for the person who wants to be involved in the Deaf community. It's for the person who has Deaf or Hard of Hearing coworkers, neighbors, friends, and family members and wants to engage with and support them. It's for the student who wants to supplement or deepen their ASL instruction.

This workbook is for you.

HOW TO USE THIS BOOK

While there is an ideal way to use this workbook, there also isn't a wrong way. The chapters progress in difficulty, and you'll find signs from previous chapters repeated in later chapters. This may make jumping around from chapter to chapter slower, but it's possible.

Each chapter has three main parts:

- The main topic and concepts you'll learn

- Lessons with vocabulary, sentences, and practice exercises

- A chapter Progress Check to practice many, if not all, of the signs you've learned in that chapter

The vocabulary and sentences were hand-picked for real-world use. These are sentences that are most commonly needed and used. Lessons teach vocabulary and grammar necessary to communicate right away—they don't isolate vocabulary and grammar exercises. They are designed to help you become more comfortable communicating with your friends, family, and community right away.

Grammar 101

ASL grammar is quite different from English grammar. The word order is unique, there are no "to be" verbs, and you can alter the meaning of a sign by adjusting your facial expressions. These are just a few examples of the differences you can expect to find.

As you go through this workbook, every ASL sentence is in the correct word order. Be sure to sign these examples as they are presented to you, in that order. The best way to learn ASL grammar is through exposure to vocabulary in context. This workbook is a good place to start.

Types of Exercises

You'll find three types of practice exercises throughout the book. They will help you practice and check your understanding of signs and sentences, building your recognition of the same signs when they are signed to you.

WORD BANK

You will see a word bank of signs. Put the correct word-bank sign under the corresponding sign. Then practice each sign from the word bank in the mirror.

MULTIPLE CHOICE

There will be several questions with English sentences or words and three possible sign choices for the correct answer. Choose the correct sign to match the English word.

FILL IN

There are two types of fill-in questions: The first one is for vocabulary. You'll see the sign and be prompted to write its name underneath. The second is for phrases and sentences. The signs will be presented in a complete thought, and you will write the signs below it to create a complete sentence.

Things to Keep in Mind

The American Sign Language Workbook is a resource to help you begin to learn ASL. It is not a complete resource to learn every single thing you need to know in order to become a fluent signer. The good news is that you're not only going to learn signs. You will also see them in context, in phrases that showcase proper ASL grammar.

Each sign you'll learn has five parameters that you'll need to pay close attention to as you go through the book. The five parameters are hand-shape, palm orientation, location, movement, and non-manual markers. A slight difference in any one of these parameters will change the meaning of the sign.

HANDSHAPES

Each sign is composed of one, two, or more handshapes. This is the shape that your hand is in to form a sign. If you change the handshape of a sign, you can alter the meaning significantly. For instance, in WHITE and LIKE, every parameter is the same except for the handshape. There are many ASL handshapes. Here are the most common handshapes you'll see:

OPEN B

OPEN A

5

S

FLAT O

1

PALM ORIENTATION

Palm orientation means the direction your palm is facing. Your palm can face up, down, to the side, toward your body, or at a specific angle. Sometimes a sign can start with one palm orientation and move into another. Be aware of these changes.

STAR

SOCK

LOCATION

Every sign has a specific location. A sign can be in one location or more than one. It can start in one place and end in another. For instance, you sign MOM in one location, but when you sign WOMAN, it begins in one spot and moves to a second location. This is one of the most common differences between signs.

MOM

WOMAN

MOVEMENT

There are multiple types of movements your signs can make. They can be stationary, tap, twist, circle, wiggle, shake, or a combination of any of these movements. Movement is a big part of what makes signing so much fun. It really makes the visual elements pop and the picture clear.

COLD

NON-MANUAL MAKERS

"Non-manual markers" simply means all of those additional elements that are not done by the hands or arms that add meaning to the sign. Without these elements, the sign wouldn't mean the same thing. For instance, you sign NOT YET and LATE with the exact same four parameters, except you additionally stick your tongue out to the side for NOT YET. It's such a simple change with a big impact.

NOT YET

LATE

Non-manual markers can involve your mouth, your eyebrows, or your face.

Facial expressions are a vital part of sign language. Think of them as the inflection in your voice and the punctuation in your writing. Without inflection in our voices, it would be difficult to determine the true meaning of what someone says to us. Are they angry, sarcastic, tired, scared, or asking a question? It's the same with punctuation. Without it, we wouldn't know when to pause, consider, respond, or understand when a thought ended.

Non-manual markers, and facial expressions and body language in particular, are sign language's inflection and punctuation. You will learn how to use these and add them to your signing throughout this workbook. While it is important, it is also easy to master and fun.

FINGERSPELLING

Fingerspelling—using ASL letters to spell out English words—is an important aspect of ASL. There are many English words that do not have a direct sign or that use abbreviations. Proper nouns are fingerspelled. Sometimes people will fingerspell a word for emphasis. You are encouraged to master recognizing each ASL letter with ease before you start to reproduce the letters yourself. This will help you more easily understand others when they fingerspell as well as help you correctly form the letters and avoid common mistakes. In this workbook, you will see instructions to fingerspell things like places and people's names, e.g. "fs LOCATION."

SIGNING GENDER

You'll find that there are signs that are directly related to specific genders, such as MOM, DAD, GIRL, and BOY. These signs are located on specific areas of the face. Female signs are located on the bottom half of the face near the chin, and male signs are located at the top half near the forehead. Neutral gender signs are around the ear. For instance, to sign COUSIN when there is no gender referenced, you place the sign beside the ear rather than the chin or forehead.

As society has grown more inclusive to all people, no matter their gender or any other identity, you will want to be aware of these signs and be respectful to all. As the terms we use to identify people with evolve, new signs will be added to the ASL vocabulary. The best way to discover new, relevant signs is to be involved in the Deaf community. You do not have to fear asking people within the Deaf community how to sign something or their gender identification.

If you are ever in doubt about how to sign something in terms of gender or other sensitive topics, fingerspell the word you want to use rather than trying to sign it to decrease the possibility of hurting another person's feelings.

1

GETTING STARTED

In this chapter, you'll learn the first signs you need to know as you begin to communicate in American Sign Language. This vocabulary will establish a solid foundation as you build your signing skills.

At the end of this chapter, you'll know how to sign:

- The alphabet
- Numbers 1 through 1 million
- Money
- Time
- Days of the week

1.1 The Alphabet

Let's start at the beginning, with the ASL alphabet. Take care to notice the direction the hands are facing. Relax your hand as you form the letters, making sure not to squeeze your hand.

EXERCISE 1.1 FILL IN

After you have practiced the letters several times, check your recognition in the following exercise. Underneath each picture of the ASL letter, write in the correct English letter it represents. They are not in order, so pay close attention.

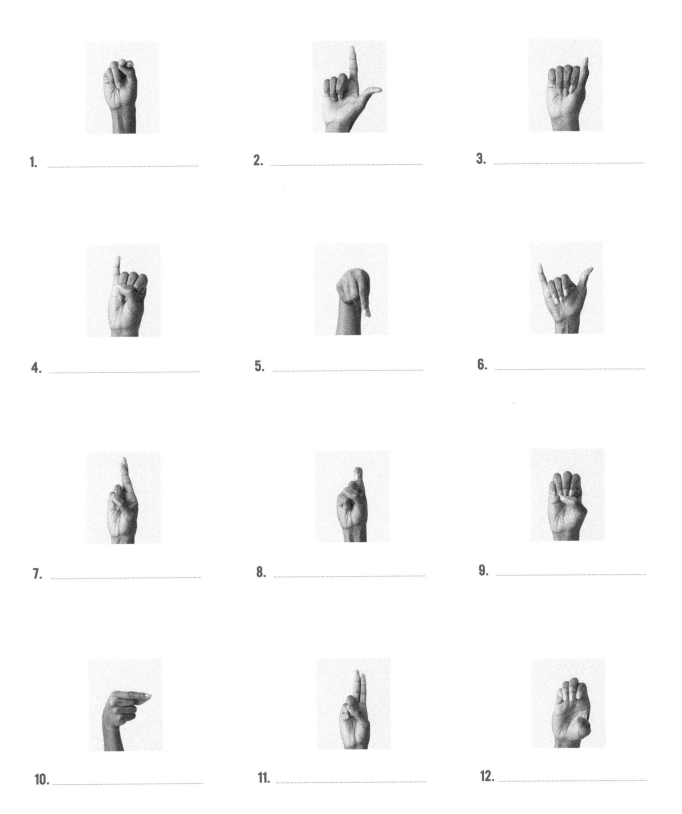

1. _____

2. _____

3. _____

4. _____

5. _____

6. _____

7. _____

8. _____

9. _____

10. _____

11. _____

12. _____

1.2 Numbers and Money

ASL numbers use only one hand rather than counting on all 10 fingers. Numbers 3, 6, 7, 8, and 9 are quite different from what you're used to. Take your time and know that you'll need to practice them often before they feel natural. For numbers that use two handshapes, the first image is the starting handshape and the second image is the ending handshape.

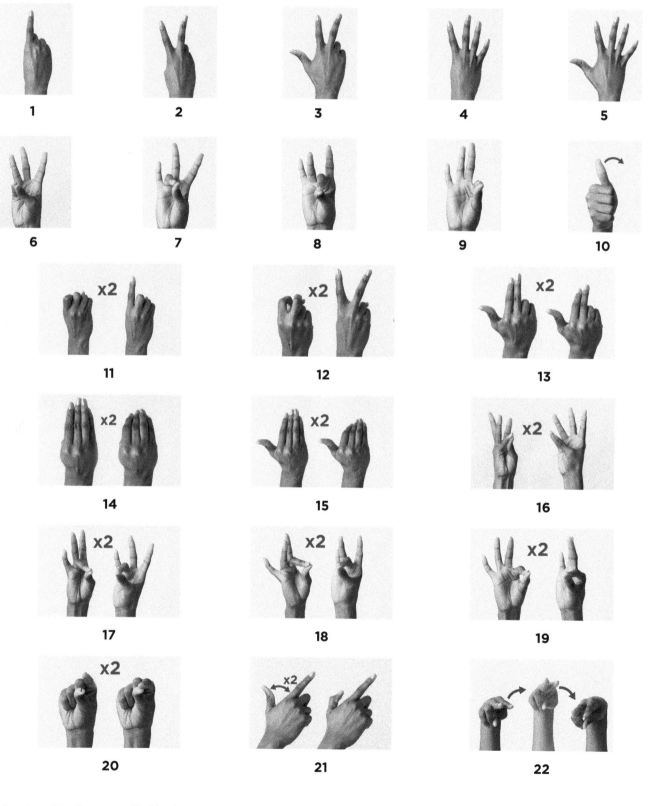

23

24

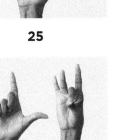

25

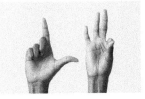

26

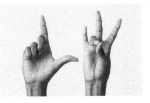

27

28

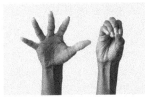

29

30

40

50

60

70

80

90

100

THOUSAND

MILLION

FRACTION

To sign a fraction, first sign the numerator. Then, holding your hand in the ending shape for the number, drag the hand down vertically, and sign the denominator.

2/3

DECIMALS

If you want to add a decimal to a number, simply sign the number, place the decimal where it belongs by using the DECIMAL sign, and then sign the remaining numbers that appear after the decimal.

9.1

DOLLAR

If you want to name the dollar amount of an item, first sign the number and then sign DOLLAR.

$23

CENT

This is a less commonly used sign, since most people will round their numbers. You can also sign cents using the decimal. Of course, signing CENT is also a great way to sign it. First sign the number and then the sign CENT.

5 CENTS

EXERCISE 1.2 MULTIPLE CHOICE

Choose the sign that matches each number.

1. 100

A.  B. 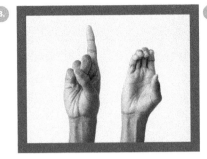 C.

2. 11

A. B. C.

3. 15

A. B. C.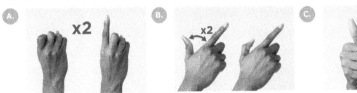

4. 7

A. B. C.

5. 3

A. B. C.

6. 25

A. B. C.

1.3 Time

In this lesson, you're going to learn how to tell time and the different times of day.

What time is it?

TIME

WHAT?

It's 2 o'clock in the afternoon.

TIME

2

AFTERNOON

I have an appointment today.

TODAY

APPOINTMENT

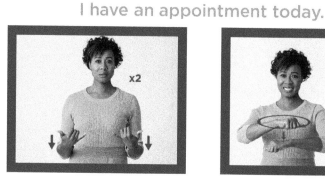
I

HAVE

RELATED VOCABULARY

MORNING

AFTERNOON

EVENING

TOMORROW

YESTERDAY

TIME: Your non-dominant hand is in the S hand-shape. Your dominant hand is in the 1 handshape, with a slight bend. Tap your finger on your wrist once, where your watch would be.

WHAT: Both hands are in the bent 5 handshape, with the palms facing up. Shake your hands side to side and furrow your eyebrows while bending your hand forward.

TIME (to tell time): To tell time, you can tap with your index finger and then drag the hand in front of your body and change to the number of the hour. Or you can tap your wrist with the number (1 through 9 only) of the hour and drag it up in front of your body, with the palm facing out.

AFTERNOON: Both hands are in the flat B hand-shape. Your non-dominant arm is held horizontally in front of the body. The forearm of the dominant hand rests on the fingertips of the non-dominant arm, with the dominant arm at a 45-degree angle.

TIME OF DAY: After you sign the number, you then sign the time of day: morning, afternoon, or night.

TODAY: Both hands are in the Y handshape, with the palms facing up. Hold the hands in front of your body and tap the hands downward two times.

APPOINTMENT: Both hands are in the A hand-shape. Hold your non-dominant hand out in front of your body, at a 45-degree angle, with the palm facing down. Hold your dominant hand just above the non-dominant hand, and circle around clockwise to form a half circle in the air. Then drop the hand down on top of the wrist of the non-dominant hand.

I: Your dominant hand is in the 1 handshape. Touch the middle of your chest with your fingertip.

HAVE: Both hands are in the bent B handshape. Bring the fingertips to your chest, right where suspenders would go. This is a firm movement.

MORNING: Both hands are in the flat B handshape. Your non-dominant arm is held horizontally in front of the body. Your dominant hand's palm is facing up. Place the fingertips of the non-dominant hand on top of the crook of the elbow of the dominant hand. Raise the dominant arm from horizontal to slightly up, just under a 45-degree angle.

NOON: Both hands are in the flat B handshape. Your non-dominant arm is held horizontally in front of the body. Place the elbow on top of the fingertips of the non-dominant hand. Your dominant arm should be vertical, with the fingertips pointed up.

EVENING: The non-dominant hand is in the flat B handshape. Your non-dominant arm is held horizontally in front of the body. The dominant hand is in the bent B handshape. Place the wrist of the dominant hand on top of the non-dominant hand, with the fingertips over the edge, pointing toward the floor.

TOMORROW: The dominant hand is in the open A handshape. Start with the thumb on the side of the cheek with the knuckles facing up. Arch the thumb off of the cheek toward the space in front of you, ending in a thumbs-up position.

YESTERDAY: The dominant hand is in the open A handshape. The palm is facing forward and the thumb is at the side of the chin, close to the cheek. Tap this spot, and in an arching movement, tap the upper cheek near the ear.

GRAMMAR TIP: TENSES

Time is an important concept in ASL. In sign language, the tense is placed at the beginning of a sentence. In English, we add tense to individual words. In ASL, we apply it to the entire sentence, using one or two signs. There are many signs that can add tense to a sentence. You can sign specific times with the signs you're learning in this chapter. However, not all situations call for specific times. In these instances, you can use general tense signs.

In ASL, the body is like a timeline. In front of your body is the future. Behind your body, or toward your back, is the past. Right on the body, or against it, is the present.

TOMORROW is signed by starting at the cheek (present) and then brought out away from the face, forward (into the future). It's just a small movement forward because tomorrow is just a few hours away.

YESTERDAY is signed starting at the front of your face (present) and then moved toward the back of the face at the ear (past). This is also a small movement backward because yesterday was just a few hours ago.

NOW or TODAY is signed with your hands held close to your stomach to indicate that it's happening at that moment on the timeline.

When you add tense to signs like WEEK, MONTH, and YEAR, you'll find that future signs start in the present and move forward, while past signs start in the present and move backward. When adding a general tense to your sentences, you can sign WILL or FUTURE for future tense, PAST or FINISH for past tense, and NOW for present.

EXERCISE 1.3 FILL IN

Identify each sign. Write the answer in the space provided below each image.

1. _____

2. _____

3. _____

4. _____

5. _____

6. _____

7. _____

8. _____

1.4 Days, Months, and Years

In this lesson, you'll learn the days of the week and the months of the year.

Are you going on Tuesday?

TUESDAY

YOU

GO?

Today's date is May 3rd.

TODAY

3

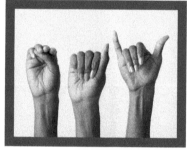

MAY

Let's have lunch this week.

NOW

WEEK

US-TWO

(LUNCH) EAT-NOON

HAVE

RELATED VOCABULARY

DAY

MONTH

YEAR

SUNDAY

MONDAY

TUESDAY

WEDNESDAY

THURSDAY

FRIDAY

SATURDAY

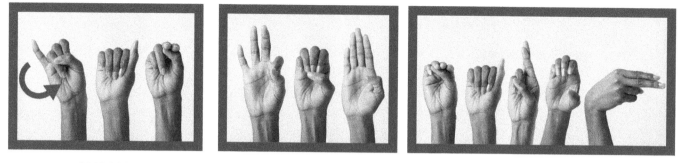

JANUARY

FEBRUARY

MARCH

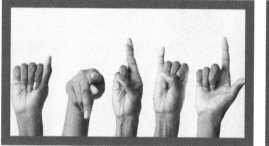

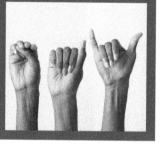

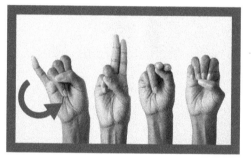

APRIL

MAY

JUNE

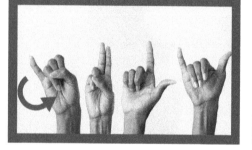

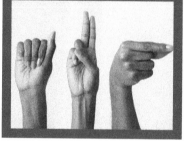

JULY

AUGUST

SEPTEMBER

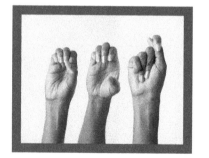

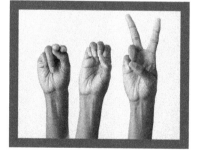

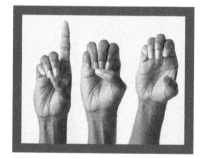

OCTOBER

NOVEMBER

DECEMBER

YOU: The dominant hand is in the 1 handshape. Point toward the person you are referring to.

GO: Both hands are in the 1 handshape. Start with both hands held vertically and angled to the side of your dominant hand. In a sharp movement, bring them both down at the same time, ending with your palms facing the ground.

TODAY (today's date): To tell the date, you sign TODAY and then sign the day of the week, the month, the day's number, and then YEAR plus the year number. You can do this full-length version of the date or sign only the important details, leaving out the rest.

NOW: This is done the same way that you sign TODAY, with both hands in the Y handshape and the palms facing up, except you bring the hands down quickly and only once.

WEEK: The non-dominant hand is in the flat B handshape, with the dominant hand in the 1 handshape and the palm facing up. Place the dominant hand on the palm of the non-dominant hand and slide the hand down the palm toward the fingertips.

US-TWO: The dominant hand is in the 2 handshape, with the palm facing up and held in front of the body. Move your hand back and forth to indicate toward the person you're talking to with your index finger and your middle finger pointed toward yourself.

(LUNCH) EAT-NOON: Lunch is a combination sign. You sign it first by signing EAT and then NOON. Sign EAT once with the flat O handshape brought to your lips once and then quickly sign NOON.

DAY: Hold your non-dominant arm in front of your body in the flat B handshape. Place your dominant hand in the 1 handshape, with the elbow on top of the fingers of your non-dominant hand. With your palm facing the side, bring the hand down in a fluid arching movement to land on top of the arm of your non-dominant hand.

MONTH: Both hands are in the 1 handshape. Your non-dominant hand is vertical with the palm facing out. The dominant hand is horizontal with the palm facing you. In a downward movement, drag the dominant hand down the non-dominant hand.

YEAR: Both hands are in the S handshape. Place the dominant hand on top of the non-dominant hand, with both hands held horizontally. Circle the dominant hand forward and around the non-dominant hand to land back on top of the non-dominant hand.

SUNDAY: Both hands are in the open B handshape. Hold the hands up in front of your body, at eye level. Circle both hands in opposite directions. The circles are small.

MONDAY: The dominant hand is in the M handshape, with the palm facing toward you. Circle the M in a counterclockwise motion.

TUESDAY: The dominant hand is in the T handshape, with the palm facing toward you. Circle the T twice in a counterclockwise motion.

WEDNESDAY: The dominant hand is in the W handshape with the palm facing toward you. Circle the W in a counterclockwise motion.

THURSDAY: The dominant hand first forms a T and then shoots out into the H handshape, with the palm facing toward you. Circle the H in a tiny circle away from your body.

FRIDAY: The dominant hand is in the F handshape with the palm facing toward you. Circle the F in a counterclockwise motion.

SATURDAY: The dominant hand is in the S handshape, with the palm facing toward you. Circle the S in a counterclockwise motion.

JANUARY: Fingerspell the letters J-A-N.

FEBRUARY: Fingerspell the letters F-E-B.

MARCH: Fingerspell the entire word.

APRIL: Fingerspell the entire word.

MAY: Fingerspell the entire word.

JUNE: Fingerspell the entire word.

JULY: Fingerspell the entire word.

AUGUST: Fingerspell the letters A-U-G.

SEPTEMBER: Fingerspell the letters S-E-P-T.

OCTOBER: Fingerspell the letters O-C-T.

NOVEMBER: Fingerspell the letters N-O-V.

DECEMBER: Fingerspell the letters D-E-C.

EXERCISE 1.4 WORD BANK

Pair each sign with the correct word. When you're finished, practice each of the word bank signs in the mirror. Hint: There are more word-bank words than there are lined spaces.

YOU	MONTH	FEBRUARY	SUNDAY
GO	YEAR	WEDNESDAY	MONDAY
TODAY	DAY	SATURDAY	DECEMBER

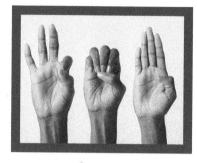

1. _____

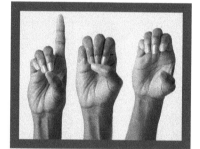

2. _____

3. _____

4. _____

5. _____

6. _____

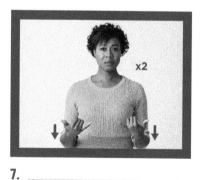

7. _____

8. _____

9. _____

10. _____

11. _____

CHAPTER 1 PROGRESS CHECK

Look at the phrases below, all made up of the signs you've learned so far in chapter 1. Identify the signs that make up each phrase. Write the answer in the spaces provided below each series of images. Afterward, practice signing each phrase using the correct facial expressions.

PHRASE 1

1. _____

2. _____

3. _____

4. _____

5. _____

PHRASE 2

6. _____

7. _____

8. _____

9. _____

10. _____

11. _____

12. _____

13. _____

14. _____

15. _____

16. _____

17. _____

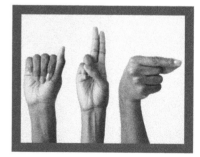

18. _____

19. _____

2

GREETINGS, FRIENDS!

In this chapter, you'll learn how to greet, meet, and chat with your friends. You'll focus on communicating around various activities and get-togethers. You'll learn things like:

- How to introduce yourself to others
- "I'm still learning, please sign slowly."
- "Do you want to grab dinner?"
- Invitations and parties
- Social activities

2.1 Introductions

The introduction is important in the Deaf community. Members of the Deaf community value connections and knowing who they are signing with. In this section, you will learn a basic introduction and how to customize it to fit you.

My name is . . .

MY

NAME

fs **NAME**

What's your name?

YOUR

NAME

WHAT?

I'm 23 years old.

I

AGE/OLD

23

RELATED VOCABULARY

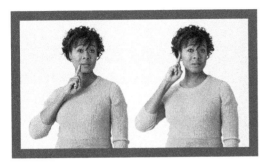

DEAF

HEARING

HARD OF HEARING

LIVE (ADDRESS)

HELLO

MY: Your dominant hand is in the flat B hand-shape and you place it on your chest, just under the collarbone.

NAME: Both hands are in the H handshape. Hold both hands horizontally forming an X shape with your dominant hand on top of the non-dominant hand's fingers. Tap the dominant hand twice.

YOUR: Your dominant hand is the flat B handshape. Hold the hand out at a slight angle with the palm pointing toward the person you're referencing.

AGE/OLD: The dominant hand starts in a tight C handshape at the chin. The chin is slightly inside the hold the hand makes around it. Pull the hand downward and squeeze the hand closed to end in an S handshape.

How to sign age: You will sign OLD, and in one fluid movement from the ending S handshape, curve the hand up and in front of your body and then sign the number.

DEAF: The dominant hand is in the 1 handshape with the palm facing out. Tap the fingertip at the side of the chin and arch back and tap in front of

the ear on the cheek. You can also see this signed from the ear to the chin.

HEARING: The dominant hand is in the 1 hand-shape, the finger held horizontally in front of the lips. Circle the finger out away from the lips twice.

HARD OF HEARING: Holding the dominant hand in the H handshape and in front of the body, tap the H once, and then make a small arch, move it out away, and tap one more time.

LIVE (ADDRESS): Both hands are in the open A handshape. Place the palm sides of the hands at the waist and bring them up, against the body, to your shoulders. Once they reach the shoulder area, they are no longer touching the body but are just in front of it.

HELLO: Your dominant hand is in the open B handshape. Place the side of the index finger to the side of the forehead and bring your hand up and out as if saluting.

EXERCISE 2.1 FILL IN

You are going to practice a pretend introduction. Fill in the name of the signs below, and sign the introduction. You can create your personalized sign by changing the information to your own. Practice this several times so that you can be comfortable introducing yourself.

1. _____

2. _____

3. _____

fs AMY

4. _____

5. _____

6. _____

7. _____

8. _____

9. _____

2.2 I'm Still Learning

People in the Deaf community love to ask how long you've been learning sign language. This lesson will help you share that information and assist you in discussing your ASL progress when you first meet another signer.

I am starting to learn ASL.

ASL

I

START

LEARN

Please sign slowly.

SIGN

SLOW

PLEASE

UP-UNTIL-NOW

I

SIGN

DAY/MONTH/YEAR

RELATED VOCABULARY

NEW

TRY

HELP

IMPROVE

WANT

ASL: You will fingerspell the three letters, A-S-L, but you want to do this in one smooth motion with the L coming out in a flicking motion.

START: The non-dominant hand is in the 5 hand-shape, with the dominant hand in the 1 handshape. Place the index finger in the webbing between the index and middle finger of the non-dominant hand. Twist your finger outward once, as if you were starting your car and your finger represented your keys.

LEARN: The non-dominant hand is in the flat B handshape and the dominant hand starts in the open B handshape. Place them palm to palm, with your dominant hand on top. Pull your dominant hand up, bringing it to your forehead. As you pull your hand up, change the handshape into the flat O. Your hand will end with the fingertips on the forehead.

SIGN: Both hands are in the 1 handshape, held in front of your body with the fingers pointing toward one another, with the hands held at a 45-degree angle. Circle your fingers toward your body in an alternating pattern.

SLOW: Both hands are in the 5 handshape. Place your dominant hand on top of your non-dominant hand. Drag the hand up until your fingertips are near the wrist of your non-dominant hand. This motion is done somewhat slowly. To demonstrate the degree of slowness, slow down the movement.

PLEASE: Your dominant hand is in the open B handshape. Place it on your chest, underneath your collarbone, and circle your hand starting in a downward motion.

UP-UNTIL-NOW: Both hands are in the 1 hand-shape. Place the fingertips of your index fingers at your shoulder of your dominant side. Arch your fingers up and forward in an exaggerated motion, ending with your hands in front of your body.

NUMBER PLUS TIME PERIOD: To sign this phrase, you first sign the number for the amount of time and then sign either DAY, MONTH, or YEAR, depending on the length of time.

NEW: The non-dominant hand is in the open B handshape, and the dominant hand is in the bent B handshape. Using your dominant hand, make a scooping motion on the palm of your non-dominant hand, leading with the fingertips and going in the direction of the length of your non-dominant hand.

TRY: Both hands are in the S handshape. Start with both hands in front of your body, with the palms facing you. Twist your wrists and swoop the hands down and up in a downward arching motion, ending with the palms facing out.

HELP: The non-dominant hand is in the open B handshape, and the dominant hand is in the open A handshape. Your non-dominant palm is facing up in front of your body, and you place your dominant hand on the palm in the thumbs-up position. Raise your non-dominant hand twice.

IMPROVE: The dominant hand is in the open B handshape, while the non-dominant arm is held out in front of the body, palm facing down. The dominant hand, with its palm facing you, is placed on the wrist of the non-dominant hand. Bounce the right hand up the left arm in small increments.

WANT: Both hands are in the bent 5 handshape, palms facing up and in front of the body. Pull your hands toward the body, as if opening a drawer.

EXERCISE 2.2 MULTIPLE CHOICE

Choose the correct sign to match each word.

1. PLEASE

A.

B.

C.

2. SLOW

A.

B.

C.

3. HELP

A.

B.

C.

4. LEARN

A.

B.

C.

2.3 Meeting Up

In this lesson, you'll learn how to invite your family and friends out for a variety of fun activities.

Do you want to go eat dinner?

DINNER

YOU

WANT

GO

EAT?

We're watching a movie tonight.

TONIGHT

MOVIE

PHRASE CONTINUES>

WE

WATCH

Do you want to go on a hike on Saturday?

SATURDAY

HIKE

YOU

WANT?

RELATED VOCABULARY

STORE

SHOPPING

DANCE

GAME

CHAT

DINNER: Dinner is a combination sign. You sign it first by signing EAT and then NIGHT. Sign EAT once with the flat O handshape brought to your lips and quickly sign NIGHT.

EAT: Bring your dominant hand, in a flat O handshape, directly to your lips once.

TONIGHT: Tonight is a combination sign of NOW and NIGHT. Sign them together, quickly and smoothly.

MOVIE: The non-dominant hand is in the flat B handshape, palm facing in, and the dominant hand is in the 5 handshape, palm facing out. Place the dominant hand behind the non-dominant hand and shake the dominant hand back and forth.

WE: Your dominant hand is in the 1 handshape, with the palm facing in. Place the index finger on the dominant side of your chest. Arch your finger across to the non-dominant side of your chest.

WATCH: Your dominant hand is in the bent L handshape in front of your body, palm up. Bring the hand forward in a single movement.

HIKE: Both hands are in the 3 handshape, palms facing down. Move the hands forward in an alternating pattern, mimicking feet taking steps.

STORE: Both hands are in the flat O handshape, palms facing down and in front of your body. Flick your wrists up twice.

SHOPPING: The non-dominant hand is in the open B handshape, palm facing up and in front of the body. The dominant hand is in the flat O handshape, palm facing up and on top of the palm of your non-dominant hand. Slide your dominant hand down and off the non-dominant hand twice. It's a small and quick movement.

DANCE: The non-dominant hand is in the open B handshape, palm facing up and in front of the body. The dominant hand is in the 2 handshape, fingertips pointing down toward the center of the palm of the non-dominant hand. With the hand above but not touching the palm, move the fingers side to side by twisting your wrist.

GAME: Both hands are in the open A handshape, palms facing in and held apart, in front of the body. Bring both hands together, tapping the flat areas together twice.

CHAT: Both hands are in the bent 5 handshape, palms angled up. Shake both hands down at an angle twice.

GRAMMAR TIP: ASKING A QUESTION

There are two main ways to ask questions in ASL. If you are asking WH-questions—questions that begin with "who," "what," "where," "when," or "why"—furrow your eyebrows and tilt your head forward. You will place the questions word (e.g., "what") at the end of the sentence.

If you want to ask a yes/no question, place the question sign at the end of the sentence and raise your eyebrows. Hold the sign for a beat longer than you normally would. For yes/no questions, any sign can be the question sign—it depends on what you are asking. In the lesson on the previous page, EAT and WANT are both question signs. EAT is a question sign because we want to know if the other person wants to grab a bite to eat; WANT is a question sign because you are inquiring if that's something the other people would like to do. Both are correct in this case.

EXERCISE 2.3 FILL IN

Identify each sign. Write the answer in the space provided below each image.

1. ....

2. ....

3. ....

4. ....

5. ....

6. ....

2.4 Throwing a Party!

In this lesson, you'll gain a basic understanding of how to communicate about a party you're hosting or attending.

I emailed you the invitation.

INVITE

EMAIL

I

SEND

Will you and your partner be able to make it?

YOU

AND

PARTNER

COME

ABLE?

How many people are attending?

PEOPLE

ATTEND

HOW-MANY?

RELATED VOCABULARY

PARTY   **WELCOME**   **FOOD**

BEER

WINE

INVITE (WELCOME/HIRE): Your dominant hand is in the open B handshape, palm facing up. Hold the hand out away from your body, off to the dominant side of your body. Bring the hand in toward your torso.

EMAIL: The non-dominant hand is in the flat C handshape, palm facing the side. Your dominant hand is in the 1 handshape, palm facing down. Pass the index finger through the space of your C hand from the back to the front. This motion is done once.

FINISH: Both hands are in the 5 handshape, palms facing in with the hands up in front of the shoulder area. Flip your wrists out toward the sides, ending with your palms facing out.

SEND: The non-dominant hand is in the open B handshape, palm facing down and in front of the body. The dominant hand starts in the bent B handshape, with the fingertips on the back of the non-dominant hand. Flick the fingertips off, ending with your dominant hand in the open B handshape.

AND: The dominant hand starts in the 5 handshape, palm facing in. Pull the hand toward the side of the dominant hand, closing the 5 handshape into the flattened O handshape.

PARTNER: Both hands are in the bent 5 handshape, palms facing in. Bring the hands together in front of your body, interlocking your fingers.

SPOUSE: Spouse is a combination sign of HUSBAND and WIFE, signed in rapid succession. This is used no matter the gender of either partner, same- or opposite-gender partners, etc. You sign HUSBAND by having both hands in the open C handshape. The non-dominant hand is palm up in front of the body and the dominant hand is palm facing out, starting at the side of the forehead. Bring the dominant hand down into the clasp of the non-dominant hand. WIFE is done the same, except the dominant hand starts at the side of the chin. To sign SPOUSE, you sign them together quickly, with no pause between the two signs.

COME: This is the opposite of GO. Both hands are in the 1 handshape, palms facing up and fingers pointing off the side at an angle. Arch the fingertips of the index fingers up and end pointing toward yourself.

ABLE: Both hands are in the S handshape, palms facing down, and in front of the body. Tap both hands down in a short, quick movement and then arch the hands in a small arch toward the right, ending in a second tap.

PEOPLE: Both hands are in the P handshape, palms facing down and in front of the body. Circle the hands out, alternating your hands.

ATTEND: This is GO signed twice. Both hands are in the 1 handshape. Start with both hands held vertically, the hands angled to the side of your dominant hand. In a sharp movement, bring them both down at the same time twice, ending with your palms facing the ground.

HOW-MANY?: Start with both hands in the S handshape, palms facing up and in front of the body. Open the hands upward into the loose 5 handshape. You need to furrow your eyebrows while signing this question.

PARTY: Both hands are in the Y handshape, arms held out horizontally in front of the body. Move both hands side to side in tandem.

FOOD: This is EAT signed twice. Bring the flat O handshape up to your lips and tap twice.

BEER: Both hands are in the 1-I handshape, palms facing the sides, and arms held horizontally in front of the body. Place the dominant hand on top of the non-dominant hand and tap twice.

WINE: The dominant hand is in the W handshape. Place the combined pinkie and thumb on your lower cheek and circle your hand twice.

EXERCISE 2.4 WORD BANK

Pair each sign with the correct word. When you're finished, practice each of the word bank signs in the mirror.

PEOPLE	EMAIL	SEND	FINISH
INVITE	COME	ATTEND	HOW-MANY?
PARTY	ABLE		

1. ....

2. ....

3. ....

4. ....

5. ....

6. ....

7. ....

8. ....

9. ....

CHAPTER 2 PROGRESS CHECK

Identify each sign. Write the answer in the space provided below each image.

1. ....

2. ....

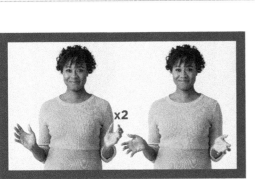

3. ....

4. ....

5. ....

6. ....

7. ....

8. ....

9. ....

11. ....

12. ....

13. ....

14. ....

15. ....

16. ....

3

FAMILY MATTERS

In this chapter, you'll get a good understanding of how to talk about family members and communicate about your interactions with them. You'll learn things like:

- Immediate family member signs
- Pet family members
- Extended family members
- Birthdays, marriages, and other special occasions

3.1 Family

In this lesson, you'll learn the signs for your immediate family.

I have __ sisters and __ brothers.

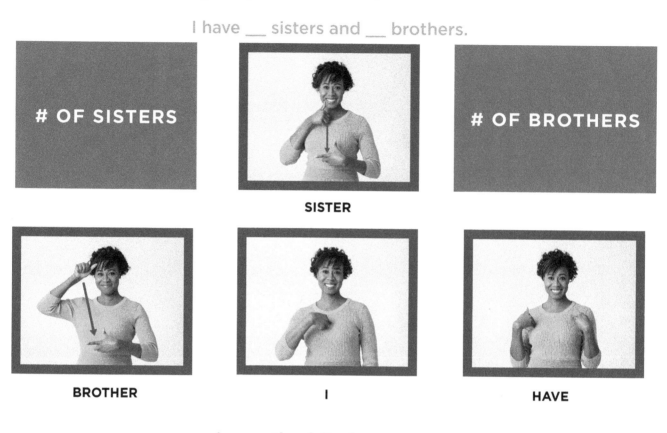

| # OF SISTERS | SISTER | # OF BROTHERS |

BROTHER

I

HAVE

I recently visited my mom.

RECENT

MY

MOM

I

VISIT

My children are flying in this weekend.

NOW

WEEKEND

MY

CHILDREN

FLY-TO

RELATED VOCABULARY

DAD

PARENT

AUNT

FAMILY

UNCLE

SISTER: The non-dominant hand begins in the A handshape, while the dominant hand is in the open A handshape. The non-dominant hand is held in front of the body, and the dominant hand's thumb is placed on the cheek, near the mouth. Bring your dominant hand down on top of the non-dominant hand. As you make this movement, both hands change into the 1 handshape.

BROTHER: The non-dominant hand begins in the A handshape while the dominant hand is in the open A handshape. The non-dominant hand is held in front of the body, and the dominant hand's thumb is placed on the side of the forehead. Bring your dominant hand down on top of the non-dominant hand. As you do this movement, both hands change into the 1 handshape.

RECENT: Your dominant hand is in the X handshape, your palm facing in. Place the side of your X on your chin near your mouth. Your mouth is open in a clenched-teeth expression.

MOM: Your dominant hand is in the 5 handshape, palm facing the side. Place your thumb on the side of your chin, just under the corner of your mouth on your dominant hand's side.

VISIT: Both hands are in the 2 handshape with your palms facing in and hands held in front of the body. Circle your hands, in an alternating motion, toward your body two times. These are small- to medium-sized circles.

WEEKEND: Your non-dominant hand is in the flat B handshape, palm facing up, and in front of your body. The dominant hand is in the 1 handshape, palm facing down, placed at the heel of the palm of your non-dominant hand. Slide your dominant hand down the palm toward the fingertips. When you reach the fingertips, bring your dominant hand down toward the floor.

CHILDREN: Both hands are in the flat B handshape, palms facing down, held in front of the body with the hands close together. Bounce your hands apart two times, as if you were patting the heads of several small children standing in front of you.

FLY: Your dominant hand is in the I-L handshape. Your palm is angled down, and your hand is up near your shoulder. Arch your hand forward to simulate a flying motion.

DAD: Your dominant hand is in the 5 handshape, palm facing the side. Place your thumb on the side of your forehead on your dominant hand's side.

SIBLING: The sign is made by signing either BROTHER or SISTER. There is no separate sign for it. If you want to ask someone if they have siblings, you can sign: BROTHER SISTER YOU-HAVE?

AUNT: Your dominant hand is in the A handshape. Hold it near the side of your cheek near your chin but not touching your face, palm facing out. Circle out with two very small circling motions.

UNCLE: Your dominant hand is in the U handshape. Hold it near the side of your forehead but not touching your face, palm facing out. Circle out with two very small circling motions.

PARENT: This is the combination of MOM and DAD. You will sign MOM and then DAD in one smooth motion, tapping the chin and then the forehead. This sign is to be used for one parent or more than one parent, regardless of gender.

FAMILY: Both hands are in the F handshape, palms facing out, with the tips of your thumbs and index fingers together in front of your body. Circle your hands around to have your pinkies touch, with your palms facing in.

PETS!

Beloved pets are family members, too. Here are some of the most common pets.

DOG

CAT

BIRD

FISH

DOG: Your dominant hand is in the K handshape, palm facing up, held on your dominant side. Rub your middle finger and thumb together as if snapping.

CAT: Your dominant hand is in the F handshape, palm facing out. Place the circled fingers at the corner of your mouth and pull out.

BIRD: Your dominant hand is in the G handshape, held against the side of the cheek with the fingers near the mouth. Pinch your index finger and thumb together twice.

FISH: Your dominant hand is in the open B handshape, palm facing the side, with the hand horizontal. Bend your hand twice while moving it forward quickly. You're showing the tail moving side to side.

EXERCISE 3.1 MULTIPLE CHOICE

Choose the correct sign to match each word.

1. SISTER

2. FAMILY

3. CHILDREN

4. VISIT

3.2 Relatives

In this lesson, you'll learn the signs for extended family members and some related vocabulary.

My father-in-law is retiring soon.

SOON

MY

FATHER-IN-LAW

HE

RETIRE

His cousin _____ is moving to Japan.

HIS

COUSIN (male)

fs NAME

PHRASE CONTINUES>

JAPAN

HE

MOVE

Where do your grandparents live?

YOUR

GRANDMA

GRANDPA

LIVE

WHERE?

RELATED VOCABULARY

COUSIN (female)

COUSIN (neutral)

MOTHER-IN-LAW

SOON: Your dominant hand is in the F handshape, palm facing in and hand held horizontally. Place the circled fingers on your chin, just underneath your bottom lip. Your mouth is in a pursed O shape, as if you were blowing out your candles.

FATHER-IN-LAW: This is a combination sign of both DAD and LAW. You first sign DAD and then smoothly transition to sign LAW. You sign LAW with your non-dominant hand in the flat B handshape held vertically in front of your body, with the palm facing the side. Your dominant hand is in the L handshape, palm facing the other hand. Place the dominant hand on the palm of your other hand near the top, and then tap the bottom of the non-dominant hand. Tap at the top then at the bottom.

RETIRE: Both hands are in the 5 handshape, with the palms facing the sides. Place your thumbs on your chest, near the shoulders, where you'd have suspenders. Tap your thumbs two times on this spot. The remaining fingers on both hands are pointed inward toward one another.

HIS: This is the sign for YOUR, but you are holding it off to the side, or pointing your palm in the direction of the person you are referring to. This sign can mean HIS, HER, YOUR, or ITS.

COUSIN (male): Your dominant hand is in the C handshape, palm facing the side. Hold the hand near the forehead at the side of the head but not touching. Circle the hand twice in small circles.

JAPAN: Both hands start in the bent L handshape, with your palms facing the sides and hands held horizontally. Place the index fingers and thumbs of both hands together in front of your body. In this position, they form a sort of rectangle. Pull your hands away from each other, and as you do, pinch your fingertips together to form two flat Os with your index fingers and thumbs.

MOVE: Both hands are in the flat O handshape, palms facing down, with hands in front of the body. Arch your hands toward the dominant side of your body.

GRANDMA: Start out by signing MOM, and arch your hand out in two small arches away from your face.

GRANDPA: Start out by signing DAD, and arch your hand out in two small arches away from your face.

LIVE: Both hands are in the open A handshape. Place them on your waist with the thumbs pointed up. Drag your hands up your body, ending near your shoulders. Once you reach this area, your hands will no longer be on your body but slightly away from it.

WHERE: Hold your dominant hand up in the 1 handshape, with the palm facing out. Shake your finger side to side while furrowing your eyebrows and tilting your head.

COUSIN (female): Your dominant hand is in the C handshape, with the palm facing the side. Hold the hand near the cheek at the side of the mouth but not touching. Circle the hand twice in small circles.

COUSIN (neutral): Your dominant hand is in the C handshape, with the palm facing the side. Hold the hand near the ear at the side of the head but not touching. Circle the hand twice in small circles.

MOTHER-IN-LAW: This is a combination sign of both MOM and LAW. You first sign MOM and then smoothly transition to sign LAW. You sign LAW with your non-dominant hand in the flat B handshape, held vertically in front of your body with the palm facing the side. Your dominant hand is in the L handshape, with the palm facing the other hand. Place the dominant hand on the palm of your other hand near the top, and then tap the bottom of the non-dominant hand. Tap at the top and then at the bottom.

EXERCISE 3.2 WORD BANK

Pair each sign with the correct word. When you're finished, practice each of the word bank signs in the mirror.

SOON	RETIRE	GRANDPA	LIVE
MOTHER-IN-LAW	JAPAN	MOVE	FATHER-IN-LAW
GRANDMA	COUSIN		

1. _____

2. _____

3. _____

4. _____

5. _____

6. _____

7. _____

8. _____

9. _____

10. _____

3.3 Special Occasions

In this lesson, you'll learn how to communicate about some special occasions that happen in our lives.

My sister is getting married this weekend.

NOW

WEEKEND

MY

SISTER

SHE

MARRY

I'm sorry to hear you were at a funeral.

RECENT

YOU

ATTEND

FUNERAL

I

SORRY

LAST-WEEK

MY

SON

BECOME

2-YEARS-OLD

RELATED VOCABULARY

BIRTHDAY   **WEDDING**   **ANNIVERSARY**

MARRY: Both hands are in the C handshape in front of your body. The dominant hand is angled down and out, and the non-dominant hand is angled up and in. Bring the hands together.

SORRY: Your dominant hand is in the S hand-shape. Place it on your chest and move it in a circle toward your non-dominant side.

FUNERAL: Both of your hands are in the 2 hand-shape, with the palms facing out. Place your dominant hand in front, and the non-dominant hand behind the dominant hand but not touching.

Bounce the hands forward, keeping your face somber or sad.

SON: Both hands are in the flat B handshape. Your non-dominant hand is palm facing up, in front of your body, as if holding a baby. The dominant hand starts by touching the side of the forehead with the side of your index finger and the palm is facing down. Bring the dominant hand down on top of the non-dominant arm, landing palm facing up.

BECOME: Both hands are in the flat B handshape, with the palms together, and each hand starting in opposite angles. Your dominant hand begins with the fingertips angled toward your body, and the non-dominant hand angled away from the body. Twist both wrists simultaneously to switch angles.

AGES 1–9: To sign any age from years 1 through 9, you begin the sign with the number of the age on the tip of the chin and swoop it down and up. If the age is above 9, you use the original method of signing OLD and then transition into the number as you bring the hand down and up.

LAST-WEEK: The non-dominant hand is in the flat B handshape, and the dominant hand is in the 1 handshape. Hold the non-dominant hand with the palm facing up and in front of the body. Start with your dominant hand with the palm facing down at the heel of the non-dominant hand. Bring your hand down the palm, toward the fingertips. As you reach the fingertips, bring your dominant hand back toward your shoulder, and twist the palm to face your body.

BIRTHDAY: Your dominant hand is in the 5 hand-shape, with the middle finger extended forward. Place the tip of your middle finger on the center of your chin and then bring it down to touch your chest, around your collarbone.

WEDDING: Both hands are in the open B hand-shape, with the palms facing in. Your hands are in front of your body, with the fingertips angled down and out. Bring the hands together in an arching motion, with the dominant hand overlapping the non-dominant hand.

ANNIVERSARY: Both hands are in the baby O handshape, with the palms facing in and hands above the shoulders. Circle your hands around in the air and smile.

Identify each sign. Write the answer in the space provided below each image.

1. ....

2. ....

3. ....

4. ....

5. ....

6. ....

7. ....

8. ....

9. ....

10. ....

11. ....

12. ....

CHAPTER 3 PROGRESS CHECK

Identify the signs that make up each phrase. Write the answer in the spaces provided below each series of images.

PHRASE 1

1. ....

2. ....

3. ....

4. ....

5. ....

PHRASE 2

6. ....

7. ....

8. ....

9. ....

10. ....

11. ....

4
EMOTIONS

Emotions are a large part of our lives. They are a part of daily communication with everyone we encounter. In this chapter, you'll learn how to express and share basic emotions so that your meaning is clear. You'll learn things like:

- Happy and sad
- Frustrated, scary, upset (and other challenging emotions)
- Wonderful, funny, excited (and other positive emotions)

4.1 Basic Feelings

In this lesson, you'll gain a basic understanding of how to communicate your most common emotions. Remember, it's very important that you use your facial expressions to match the emotions you sign.

That made me so happy.

THAT

INFLUENCE-me

HAPPY

I feel upset.

I

FEEL

UPSET

That was really scary.

THAT

HAPPEN

TRUE/REALLY

SCARE

RELATED VOCABULARY

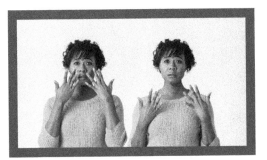

SAD

WONDERFUL

ANGRY

EXCITED

FRUSTRATED

THAT: There is a generic and specific way to sign THAT. For the general, your dominant hand is in the Y handshape, and your non-dominant hand is in the flat B handshape, with the palm facing up. Place the Y hand into the palm of your non-dominant hand. To sign THAT specifically, only use your dominant hand and aim your palm in the direction of the subject you're referencing. Your palm starts out and ends facing down.

INFLUENCE-me: Your non-dominant hand is in the flat B handshape, held horizontally in front of the body, with the palm facing down. Your dominant hand begins in the flat O handshape, with the fingertips on the back of the non-dominant hand. The fingertips are pointed out away from

the body. Slide your dominant hand forward off of the non-dominant hand. As you slide your hand, open your dominant hand into the 5 handshape.

HAPPY: Your dominant hand is in the open B handshape, with the palm facing in. Brush your hand up your chest in a circular motion twice. As you sign HAPPY, smile or otherwise look happy.

FEEL: Your dominant hand is in the 5 handshape with the middle finger extended forward. Your palm is facing in. Brush your hand up your chest in a circular motion twice. You are making contact with your chest with your extended middle finger only.

UPSET: Your dominant hand is in the open B handshape with the palm facing down and the side of your thumb and hand resting on your stomach. Flip your hand over and end with your palm facing up and the edge of your pinky on your stomach. As you sign this, pull the corners of your mouth down.

TRUE/REALLY: Your dominant hand is in the 1 handshape, with the palm facing to the side. Start the sign with the side of your fingertip on your chin. Slide your hand up and out in an arch.

HAPPEN: Both hands are in the 1 handshape, held horizontally in front of the body with the palms facing each other. Twist your wrists to bring the hands down, with the palms facing down. Repeat this movement twice.

SCARE: Both of your hand begin in the S handshape, with the palms facing the body and the hands horizontal. Move your hands in toward each other, and as you do, open both hands into the 5 handshape. Open your mouth in a wide O shape as you sign SCARE.

SAD: Both hands are in the 5 handshape, with the palms facing in, hands starting just underneath the eyes. Bring the hands straight down the face, ending at the jawline. Your facial expressions are sad.

WONDERFUL: Both hands are in the open B handshape, with the palms facing out, and hands above the shoulders. Tap the air in front of your hands and then tap the air in front of your hands again but a few inches lower.

ANGRY: Your dominant hand is in the 5 handshape in front of your face, with the palm facing in. Bend your hands into the 5 claw handshape two times. Look angry.

EXCITED: Both hands are in the 5 handshape with the middle finger extended forward, with the palms facing in. Alternating between hands, brush your hands up the sides of your chest in a circular motion twice. You are making contact with your chest using your extended middle finger only.

FRUSTRATED: Your dominant hand is in the flat B handshape. Hit the tip of your chin with the back of your hand one time.

EXERCISE 4.1 WORD BANK

Pair each sign with the correct word. When you're finished, practice each of the word bank signs in the mirror.

HAPPY	SAD	EXCITED	TRUE
UPSET	WONDERFUL	FRUSTRATED	FEEL
SCARY	ANGRY		

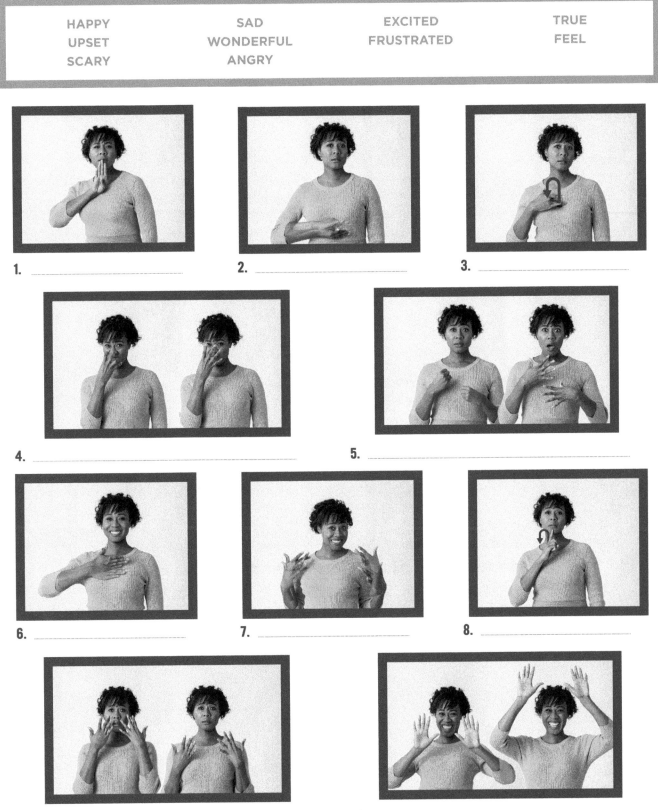

1. _____

2. _____

3. _____

4. _____

5. _____

6. _____

7. _____

8. _____

9. _____

10. _____

4.2 Difficult Emotions

In this lesson, you'll learn signs to match a variety of difficult emotions and how to communicate your feelings with others.

I'm really concerned about my dog.

MY

DOG

HIMSELF

I

CONCERN

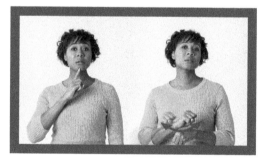

TRUE-BIZ

You look worried, how can I help?

YOU

APPEAR

WORRY

me-HELP-you

HOW?

I don't like the food there. It's lousy.

FOOD

THERE

I

DON'T-LIKE

PHRASE CONTINUES>

IT

LOUSY

RELATED VOCABULARY

CRY

BAWL

STRESS

NERVOUS

TERRIBLE

CONCERN: Both of your hands are in the 5 hand-shape, with the middle finger extended forward. Tap your chest just above your heart two times with each hand, alternating between hands. Turn the corners of your mouth down, or tighten your lips.

HIMSELF: Your non-dominant hand is in the 1 handshape, and your dominant hand in the open A handshape, with the thumb pointing up. Hold your 1 hand to the side, across your body. Tap the 1 hand twice with your open A hand. If the person or object you are referring to is near you, drop your 1 hand and tap the air with your open A hand in their direction.

TRUE-BIZ: This is an ASL idiom, or figure of speech. It means, "I really really mean it," or "It's really really true." This is a combination of the signs TRUE and BUSINESS. First sign TRUE, and then smoothly move into signing BUSINESS. To sign BUSINESS, both of your hands are in the S hand-shape. Your dominant hand will tap the edge of the non-dominant hand. You first tap right to left and then left to right.

APPEAR: Your dominant hand is in the 1 hand-shape. With the tip of your finger and the palm facing in, trace a circle around your face. You're not touching your face but just in front of it.

WORRY: Both of your hands are in the flat B hand-shape, with the palms facing out, and hands in the space in front of your forehead. In alternating circles, circle your hands down and back up two times.

me-HELP-you: HELP is a directional verb. You can sign it on its own or you can sign it with a specific direction to add to the meaning. First, let's learn the sign, and then I'll show you show to make it directional. HELP is signed with the non-dominant hand in the flat B handshape and the dominant hand in the open A handshape. Place the bottom of your open A hand, with the thumb up toward the ceiling, in the middle of your flat B hand. Raise your non-dominant hand upward in two short motions.

To make it directional, you can first sign HELP without the upward movements by holding the sign near your body and then arching it toward the person you want to help. If you want the person to help you, start the sign out from your body and arch it toward yourself.

HOW: Both hands are in the bent B handshape, with the knuckles together and palms facing in. Twist your dominant wrist to end with your palm facing up. Your eyebrows should be furrowed, and your head leaned forward slightly.

THERE: THERE is much like signing HE/SHE/IT. Your hand is in the 1 handshape, and you point off in front and to the side of you. You can point in a specific direction if it applies. If it's a general use of the sign, point off to the side of your dominant hand.

DON'T-LIKE: Start with your dominant hand in the 5 handshape against your chest. Pull your hand out as if pulling a string, and as you pull, bring your thumb and middle fingers together in the middle. This is the sign for LIKE. To make it mean DON'T-LIKE, once you've pulled your fingers out a few inches, turn your wrist out and flick your middle finger off of your thumb, as if you were flicking a piece of lint off of your shirt.

LOUSY: Your dominant hand is in the 3 hand-shape, with the tip of your thumb touching the tip of your nose. Your palm is facing the side. Bend your wrist and bring your hand slightly forward at the same time. Your palm is now facing down and your thumb is no longer on your nose. Your facial expressions should match the meaning: lousy. You can pull your lip down or scrunch your face in disgust.

CRY: Both of your hands are in the 1 handshape, with the palms facing in. Your fingertips are just under the eyes and you draw a line down both cheeks twice to show tears dripping down your face.

BAWL: Both of your hands are in the 4 handshape, with the hands horizontal and palms facing in. The tips of your index fingers are under the eyes. Draw two or three lines down the face. This shows a lot of tears streaming down your face. Your mouth needs to be open in the "ahhh" shape. This is one variation of this sign. You can also see this sign starting with the S handshapes at the sides of your face and then open into the 5 handshape, moving down and away from your face.

STRESS: Your non-dominant hand is in the S handshape, with the palm facing the side. Your dominant hand is in the 5 handshape and is on top of the S handshape. Push your S hand downward twice with your 5 hand.

NERVOUS: Both hands are in the 5 handshape, with the palms facing down and in front of your body. Shake your hands as if you are very jittery.

TERRIBLE: Both hands are in the 8 handshape, with the palms facing in and hands held up above the shoulders. Flick your thumb and middle fingers up toward the sky, and your hands ending with all fingers extended up.

GRAMMAR TIP: REMEMBER! FACIAL EXPRESSIONS

Facial expressions are a major part of ASL grammar. Think of them as punctuation in a written sentence and voice inflection in a spoken one. Your facial expressions need to match the message you're intending—without them, your message is lost.

When you start to sign, you'll be focused on producing the signs correctly; often facial expressions are forgotten. To avoid this common mistake, when you practice the signs and the sentences in this workbook, add your facial expressions at the same time. Try each sentence with a variety of facial expressions. Pick a sentence and sign it using five different emotions, for instance: worry, surprise, joy, fear, boredom. Watch yourself in the mirror and sign like no one's watching. If you practice facial expressions at the same time as you practice signing, they'll become natural and easy.

EXERCISE 4.2 MULTIPLE CHOICE

Choose the correct sign to match each word.

1. TERRIBLE

2. CRY

3. CONCERN

4.3 Positive Emotions

While we've learned several negative emotions, there are just as many positive emotions and feelings to have and share. In this lesson, you'll learn several signs to convey different types of happiness.

My daughter is really funny.

MY

DAUGHTER

SHE

TRUE

FUNNY

Did you enjoy the book?

BOOK

YOU

ENJOY?

You did it! That was incredible.

GOAL

YOU

ACCOMPLISH

SURPRISE/PAH

YOU

AWESOME

RELATED VOCABULARY

SILLY

CUTE

SWEET

NEAT

DAUGHTER: Both hands are in the flat B hand-shape. Your non-dominant hand is facing palm up in front of your body, as if holding a baby. The dominant hand starts by touching the side of the chin with the side of your index finger, and the palm is facing down. Bring the dominant hand down on top of the non-dominant arm, landing palm facing up.

FUNNY: Your dominant hand is in the U hand-shape, with the palm facing in. Brush the end of your nose twice.

BOOK: Both of your hands are in the open B hand-shape with the edges of your pinkies together in the middle. Your hands are forming the front and back covers of the book. Open and close your hands twice.

ENJOY: Both of your hands are in the open B handshape. Place your dominant hand on your chest and your non-dominant hand on your stom-ach. Circle your hands twice.

GOAL: Both of your hands are in the 1 hand-shape. Hold your non-dominant hand up, above your shoulder. Your dominant hand is held lower, with the palm facing the side. Bend your wrist so that your dominant hand finger is now pointing at the tip of your non-dominant hand. They do not touch. It's important that your non-dominant hand is higher up than your dominant hand.

ACCOMPLISH: The non-dominant hand is in the 1 handshape, held up above your head, on your

non-dominant side. Start with your dominant hand in the 5 handshape. It starts in front of your body and reaches up to the top of your 1 hand. As it reaches the top it closes into the S handshape.

SUCCESS/PAH: Both of your hands are in the 1 handshape. Place the tips of your index fingers, with the palms facing in, on the sides of your chin. In a grand motion, twist your wrists open and bring your hands up, ending with your palms facing out. As you sign this, your mouth is saying PAH, without making the sounds.

SILLY: Hold your Y hand, palm to the side, in front of your nose, and twist your wrist back and forth.

CUTE: Your dominant hand is in the U handshape, with the palm facing in. Place your U fingers on the tip of your chin and bend your fingers down to swipe down and off of your chin.

SWEET: Your dominant hand is in the open B handshape, with the palm facing in. Place your fingertips on the tip of your chin and bend your fingers down to swipe down and off of your chin.

AWESOME: Your dominant hand is in the bent 5 handshape, with the palm facing in. Hold your hand just in front of your mouth and shake your hand side to side. Open your mouth in the "ahhh" shape.

NEAT: Your dominant hand is in the X handshape, held on the cheek, near the side of the mouth. Twist your wrist forward once.

EXERCISE 4.3 FILL IN

Identify each sign. Write the answer in the space provided below each image.

1. _____

2. _____

3. _____

4. _____

5. _____

6. _____

7. _____

8. _____

CHAPTER 4 PROGRESS CHECK

Pair each sign with the correct word.

STRESS	SILLY	ANGRY	WORRY
SWEET	TERRIBLE	UPSET	INFLUENCE-me
CRY	BOOK	SAD	HIMSELF
AWESOME	ENJOY	FRUSTRATE	me-HELP-you
NERVOUS	CONCERN	EXCITE	WONDERFUL

1. ....

2. ....

3. ....

4. ....

5. ....

6. ....

7. ....

8. ....

9. ....

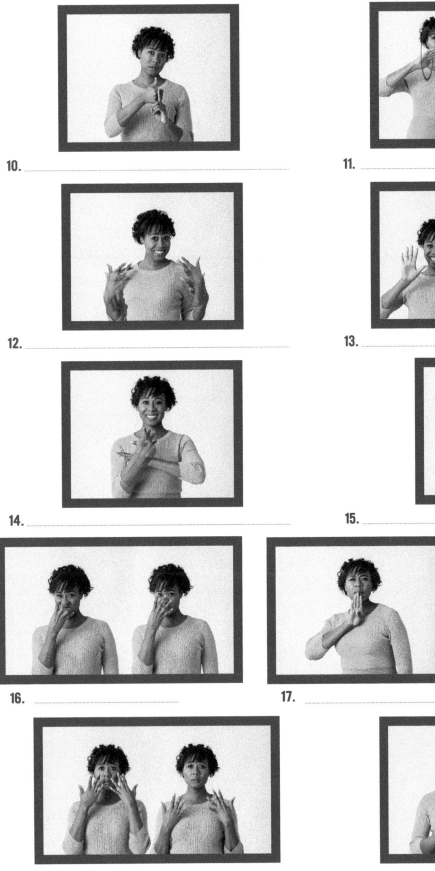

10. ....

11. ....

12. ....

13. ....

14. ....

15. ....

16. ....

17. ....

18. ....

19. ....

20. ....

5

HEALTH AND SAFETY

In this chapter, you'll gain a basic sense of how to share your health concerns and help others communicate their own health and safety challenges. You'll learn things like:

- Expressing sickness and wellness
- Personal health for women
- Describing pain and sickness
- Allergies
- Signs for emergency situations

5.1 Today, I Am . . .

In this lesson, you'll learn how to describe your health and health-related needs.

I feel sick.

MYSELF

FEEL

SICK

Which pharmacy do you use?

YOU

STORE

FOR

BUY

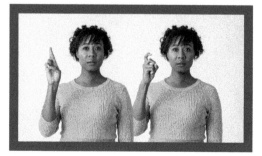

RX

MEDICINE

YOU

PREFER

WHICH?

He's taking medicine twice a day for _____.

HE

MEDICINE

take-PILL

TWICE

PHRASE CONTINUES>

DAILY

FOR-FOR?

fs AILMENT

RELATED VOCABULARY

PAIN

THROW-UP

TOOTH

DIABETES

INFECTION

MYSELF: Your dominant hand is in the open A handshape with the palm facing the side. Tap your chest twice with the back of your thumb.

SICK: Both hands are in the 5 handshape with the middle finger extended forward. Place the tip of your middle finger of your dominant hand on the side of your forehead and the tip of the middle finger of your non-dominant hand on the side of your stomach.

BUY: Your non-dominant hand is in the flat B handshape and your dominant hand is in the flat O handshape, with both palms facing up. Place the dominant hand on the palm of the non-dominant hand, and then move the hand in an arch forward, as if taking money out of your hand and handing it to the cashier.

RX: You sign the letters R and X together.

WHICH: Both hands are in the open A handshape, with the palms facing each other. Move the hands up and down in an alternating motion while furrowing the eyebrows.

MEDICINE: Your non-dominant hand is in the open B handshape, with the palm facing up, and your dominant hand is in the 5 handshape with the middle finger pushed forward. Place the tip of the middle finger in the center of the palm of your open B hand. Wiggle your dominant hand back and forth.

PREFER: Your dominant hand is in the 5 handshape with the middle finger extended forward. Tap your chin with the tip of your middle finger.

take-PILL: Your dominant hand begins in the baby O handshape. Bring your hand toward your mouth and flick your index finger open ending just before your mouth. Open your mouth slightly.

TWICE: Your non-dominant hand is in the open B handshape, with the palm facing up. Your dominant hand is in the 2 handshape. With the middle

finger of your 2 hand, scoop the palm toward your body.

DAILY: Your dominant hand is in the open A handshape, with the palm facing the side. Place the palm side along your cheek and slide it down toward your mouth twice.

FOR-FOR: Your dominant hand is in the 1 handshape, with the tip of your index finger pointing at your temple. Twist your wrist forward two times.

PAIN: Both of your hands are in the 1 handshape, with the palms facing in and hands horizontal. Bring the index fingers toward each other while simultaneously twisting in opposite directions. You can place this sign in front of any body part that hurts to show where the pain is, or sign this in front of your body to mean general pain or hurt.

THROW-UP: Both hands are in the 5 handshape with the dominant hand just in front of the mouth and the palm facing the side. The non-dominant hand is just in front of the dominant hand. Together, arch them forward and down. Your face needs to match the feeling.

TOOTH: Your dominant hand is in the X handshape with the palm facing in. Tap your teeth, just to the side of your two front teeth.

DIABETES: Your dominant hand is in the open B handshape with your palm facing in. Place your fingertips on your chin and brush your fingers down your chin three times while mouthing the word DIABETES. This is pretty much the same sign for SUGAR (though typically done twice), so you need to add the mouthing of the word for clarity.

INFECTION: Hold your dominant hand up near your shoulder in the 1 handshape. Shake the hand side to side. It's very important that you scrunch your face up in a look of disgust, otherwise it will not mean INFECTION, but INSURANCE.

EXERCISE 5.1 FILL IN

Identify each sign. Write the answer in the space provided below each image.

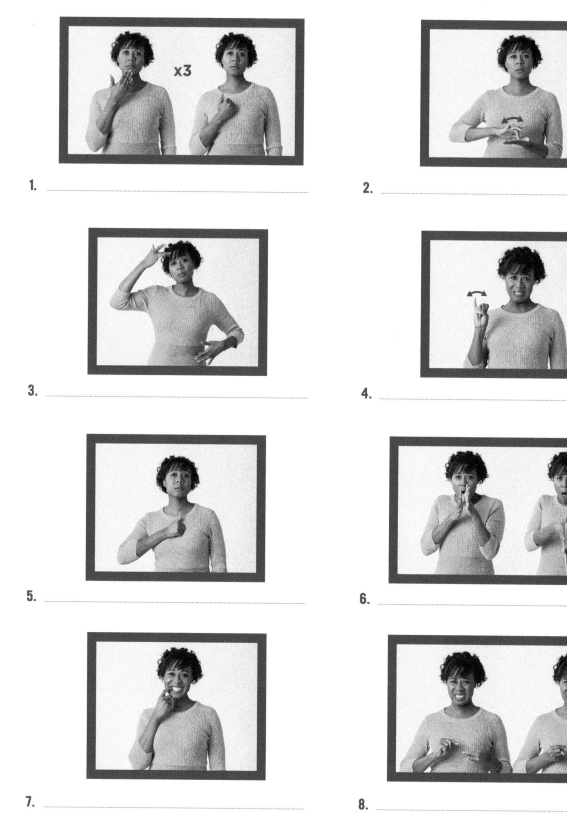

1. ....

2. ....

3. ....

4. ....

5. ....

6. ....

7. ....

8. ....

5.2 Basic Safety

In this lesson, you'll learn how to describe your basic safety needs, including the framework to convey life-threatening allergies.

I am allergic to ____.

MYSELF

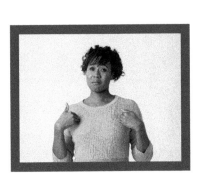

fs ALLERGEN

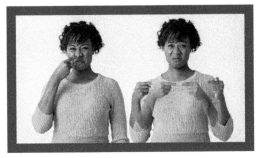

ALLERGY

HAVE

Something doesn't feel right.

SOMETHING

FEEL

RIGHT

NOT

PHRASE CONTINUES>

SOMETHING

FEEL

WRONG

He needs a doctor quickly.

DOCTOR

HE

NEED

FAST

RELATED VOCABULARY

DAIRY

NUTS

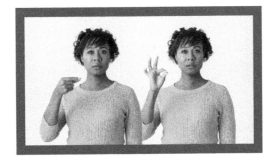

GLUTEN FREE

NURSE

BREAK

ALLERGY/ALLERGIC: This is a two-part sign. The dominant hand is in the 1 handshape, and touches the tip of your nose. In the next movement, both hands are in the G handshape, fingertips pointing toward one another. Pull your dominant hand away from the non-dominant hand in the opposite direction. Do both parts of this sign together in a fluid motion.

SOMETHING: Your dominant hand is in the 1 handshape, with the palm and the index finger facing up. Circle your hand counterclockwise. This sign has multiple meanings and is dependent on context. It can also mean: SOMEONE, SINGLE, ALONE, or ONLY.

RIGHT: Both hands are in the 1 handshape, with the hands held horizontally and at a diagonal angle in front of the body. Tap the fist of the dominant hand on top of the non-dominant hand.

NOT: The dominant hand is in the open A handshape, with the palm facing the side. Place the thumb under the chin and bring it forward and away from your body in a swift movement.

WRONG: The dominant hand is in the Y handshape, with the palm facing in. Place the 3 bent fingers on your chin and shake your head slightly in the negative.

FAST: Both hands are in the L handshape, pointing toward your dominant side at an angle. Your dominant hand is slightly in front of the non-dominant hand. Pull the index fingers back as if pulling a trigger, and your hands pop up slightly with this motion.

DAIRY/MILK: Your dominant hand is in a loose open S handshape. Squeeze it closed two times.

NUTS: This is very similar to signing NOT, but instead, place the thumb under your two front teeth and pull your open A hand out in a swift movement.

GLUTEN FREE: You fingerspell G and then quickly twist your wrist into an F. To sign GLUTEN on its own, you fingerspell the entire word.

NURSE: Your non-dominant hand is in the open B handshape and is horizontal, with your palm facing out at a 45-degree angle. Your dominant hand is in the U handshape and taps the wrist of your non-dominant hand twice.

BREAK: Both hands are in the S handshape, with the palms facing down, and your hands are together in front of your body. Twist your wrists in opposite directions, as if you were snapping a stick in half.

EXERCISE 5.2 FILL IN

Identify each sign. Write the answer in the space provided below each image.

1. ....

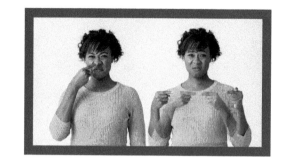

2. ....

3. ....

4. ....

5. ....

6. ....

7. ....

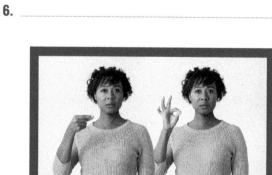

8. ....

5.3 Personal Health

In this lesson, you'll learn signs to address some common health and safety needs.

Do you have a tampon?

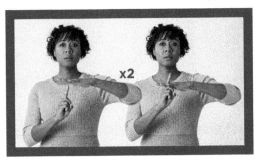

TAMPON

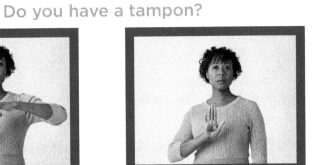

YOU

HAVE?

I don't want to walk alone.

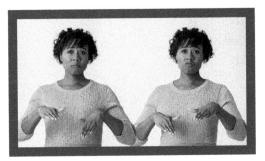

WALK

JUST-ME

I

DON'T-WANT

YOUR

DOCTOR

HE/SHE

YOUR

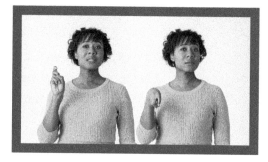

NEED

SUPPORT?

RELATED VOCABULARY

MENSTRUATE

SKIN

TEST/EXAM

BREASTFEED

SHOWER

TAMPON: Your non-dominant hand is in the Spock handshape, meaning your hand is in the open B handshape with your middle finger and index finger stuck together and your ring finger and pinky finger stuck together, but the two groups are spread apart. Hold this hand with the palm facing down and in front of your body. Your dominant hand is in the 1 handshape, and from underneath the non-dominant hand pokes up twice in the space between your fingers.

WALK: Both of your hands are in the open B handshape, palms down, in front of your body. Alternate moving your hands forward as if you were taking steps.

JUST-ME: Your dominant hand is in the 1 handshape with the palm out. Twist your wrist and bring your hand into your chest at the same time. End with your hand on your chest, with your palm facing the dominant side of your body.

DON'T-WANT: Both hands are in the bent 5 handshape, with the palms facing up and in front of your body. Pull them toward your body (this is the sign for WANT) and just before you reach your stomach, twist your hands so that your palms are facing out, and push away from yourself.

DOCTOR: Both hands are in the open B handshape. Your non-dominant hand is horizontal with your palm facing out at a 45-degree angle. Your dominant hand bends in the bent B handshape, and taps the wrist of your non-dominant hand twice.

NEED: Your dominant hand is in the X handshape, with the palm facing out and in front of your body. Bend your wrist and your palm ends facing down.

SUPPORT: Both hands as in the S handshape, with both palms facing in. The non-dominant hand is held horizontally, while the dominant hand comes up from underneath and lifts the non-dominant fist up a few inches.

MENSTRUATE: The dominant hand is in the A handshape, and taps the cheek twice.

SKIN: Using your thumb and your bent index finger, pinch your cheek.

TEST/EXAM: Both hands are in the X handshape, with the palms facing out, in front of your shoulders. Bend your index finger into the X handshape, move the hands downward, and then change your hands into the 5 handshape.

BREASTFEED: There are many variations for this sign. You first sign BREAST and then FEED. To sign BREAST, your dominant hand is in the bent B handshape and you tap above the breast on the non-dominant side and then the dominant side. Then with your non-dominant arm you hold it out as if cradling a baby. With your dominant hand you sign EAT to the area where the baby's mouth would be if it were in your arms.

SHOWER: Your dominant hand starts in the O handshape, to the side and above your head. Your open your hand up into the 5 hand, with the thumb under the 4 fingers to form a cone. Repeat this motion twice, as if the water is coming out of the shower head.

WOMEN IN THE DEAF COMMUNITY

Women have been a powerful force in the Deaf community for hundreds of years. It's important to acknowledge their achievements where history books might have overlooked them. Here are just a few:

- In 1453, **Teresa de Cartagena**, a Deaf Spanish nun, wrote two revolutionary essays: one on her deafness and its positive impact on her faith and the community and another on women's intelligence. She is heralded as Spain's first feminist writer.

- **Charlotte Elizabeth Tonna** was a British novelist and poet in the 1840s. She wrote passionately about women's rights and the importance of Deaf education. She is considered one of England's most influential writers.

- Between 1911 and 1915, astronomer **Annie Jump** developed the Harvard Classification Scheme for stars that is still used today. A brilliant "computer," she could classify any stellar spectra in under three seconds. She won prestigious awards despite men often getting credit for her work.

- **Michelle Banks** is an award-winning actress, writer, and director. In addition to her personal success in television and films, and on the stage, she also founded Onyx Theatre Company, the first Deaf theater company for people of color in the United States.

EXERCISE 5.3 MULTIPLE CHOICE

Choose the correct sign to match each word.

1. TEST

A.

B.

C.

2. ALONE

A.

B.

C.
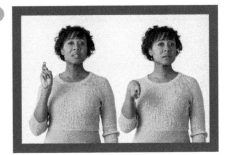

3. DOCTOR

A.

B.

C.

4. SUPPORT

A.

B.

C.

5.4 Responding to a Crisis

Emergency situations can happen, and it's best to be prepared before they do. In this lesson, you'll learn signs to help you communicate during a crisis.

Call an ambulance!

AMBULANCE

CALL

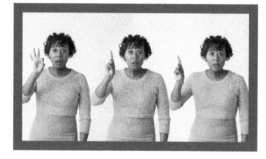

911

Where is the closest hospital?

HOSPITAL

CLOSE-BY

WHERE?

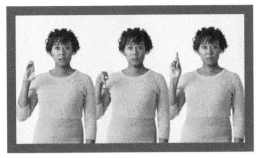

CPR

YOU-all

ANY

KNOW?

RELATED VOCABULARY

BLOOD

HEART

STROKE

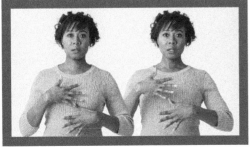

BREATH

BONE

AMBULANCE: Both hands are in the bent 5 handshape, with the palms facing out and hands above the head. Twist your wrists back and forth.

CALL: Your dominant hand is in the Y handshape, held against your cheek. Bring your hand out a few inches away from your face.

911: Fingerspell the numbers 9-1-1.

HOSPITAL: With your dominant hand in the H handshape, draw a plus sign on the side of your non-dominant arm.

CLOSE-BY: Your dominant hand is in the F handshape, with the palm facing in. Brush the tip of your circled index finger and thumb off the tip of your nose in a downward direction. As you do so, hold your mouth in a tight "ooo" shape.

CPR: Fingerspell the letters C-P-R.

YOU-all: With your dominant hand in the 1 handshape, start with the hand pointing across your body to the non-dominant side. Sweep your hand in front of your body. You can sign this generally, or begin the sign in front of the first person and end the sweep at the last person if you are referring to a specific group of people.

ANY: Your dominant hand is in the A handshape, and your palm begins the sign facing the side. Turn your hand so that it ends with the palm facing down.

KNOW: Your dominant hand is in the flat B handshape. Tap the side of your forehead at the temple. You may often see this sign done by tapping the cheekbone, for efficiency. Both are correct forms of the sign.

BLOOD: This is the combination of the sign RED, and showing liquid moving down. First sign RED with your dominant hand in the 1 handshape. Place the tip of the finger on your bottom lip, and draw a straight line down by bending your finger. The next part of the sign is done with both hands in the 5 handshape, with the palms held in and horizontal. Your non-dominant hand stays still, while the dominant hand moves from signing RED into the 5 handshape, wiggling the fingers down the non-dominant hand.

HEART: The dominant hand is in the 5 handshape, with the middle finger extended forward. Tap the area above your heart twice with the tip of your middle finger.

STROKE: The dominant hand is in the flat B handshape, and the palm faces the side. Draw a zigzagging line down the front of the body, starting at the forehead. You are just in front of your body, not touching it.

BREATH: Both hands are in the 5 handshape, held horizontally in front of the chest and stomach, with the dominant hand above the non-dominant hand. Move the hands forward, away from the body a few inches, and bring them back down to the chest. This shows the lungs expanding and contracting. To show that someone is short of breath, do this same sign, but do the movement faster and a few more times. Also, open your mouth as if gasping.

BONE: Both of your hands are in the bent V handshape, with the palms facing in. Cross your arms over each other and tap the arms together twice.

EXERCISE 5.4 MULTIPLE CHOICE

Choose the correct sign to match each word.

1. HOSPITAL

A.

B.

C.

2. AMBULANCE

A.

B.
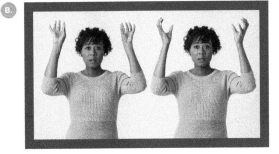

C.
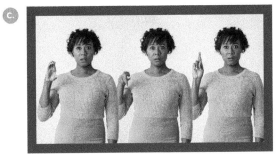

3. CALL

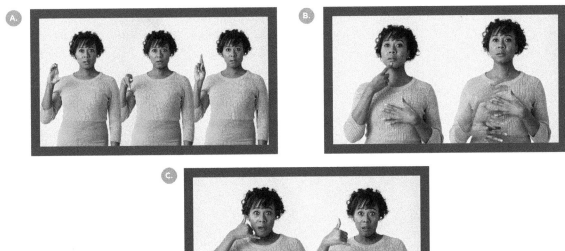

NATURAL DISASTERS

Sometimes emergency situations include natural disasters. In this section, you'll learn the signs for three common natural disasters.

EARTHQUAKE

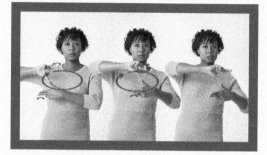

HURRICANE

TORNADO

EARTHQUAKE: First sign EARTH. Your non-dominant hand is in the S handshape, and your dominant hand in the open 8 handshape. Place the tips of your middle finger and thumb on the back of your S hand, and wiggle the hand forward and back. Next, both hands are in the S handshape, with the palms facing down. They are in front of your torso, with the hands angled toward each other. Jerk your hands quickly side to side.

HURRICANE: Both hands are in the H handshape with the thumbs extended. The palm of your non-dominant hand is facing in, and the palm of your dominant hand is facing out. Bring the thumb tips together in front of your body, with the hands horizontal. Bend your H fingers twice and move hands in a circle while signing.

TORNADO: Both hands are in the L handshape with the thumbs extended. The palm of your non-dominant hand is facing in, and the palm of your dominant hand is facing out. Bring the thumb tips together in front of your body with the hands horizontal. Bend your index fingers twice and move hands in a circle while signing.

CHAPTER 5 PROGRESS CHECK

There are two phrases below. They use signs you have learned in the previous chapters but are not phrases you've seen before. Identify the signs that make up each phrase. Write the answer in the spaces provided below each series of images.

PHRASE 1

1. ....

2. ....

3. ....

4. ....

PHRASE 2

5. ....

6. ....

7. ....

8. ....

6

WORK

In this chapter, you'll get a basic sense of how to talk about work-related topics and communicate with others on the job—whatever "work" means to you! You'll learn things like:

- Asking about jobs and careers
- Payment signs
- Office culture terminology
- Basic tech signs

6.1 What Do You Do?

In this lesson, you'll learn how to have a conversation about your livelihood and others' work as well.

What do you do for work?

YOUR

WORK

WHAT?

Did you apply for that job?

THAT

JOB

YOU

APPLY?

I work on the second floor.

MYSELF

WORK

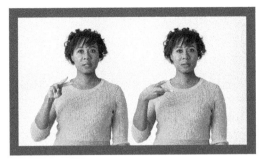

2ND

FLOOR

RELATED VOCABULARY

PAYCHECK

DEPARTMENT

MEETING

OFFICE

PHONE CALL

WORK: Both hands are in the S handshape, with the palms facing down. Tap the heel of your dominant hand on the edge of the non-dominant hand twice.

WHAT: Both hands are in the relaxed 5 handshape, with the palms facing up. Shake your hands side to side while furrowing your eyebrows and leaning your head forward.

JOB: Most often, you can sign WORK to mean job. Here is the lexicalized version of the sign, meaning it's fingerspelling in a specific way that has become a sign. To sign JOB, first sign J, and as you curve your hand in the J shape, flick your hand out into the B handshape with the palm facing toward yourself.

APPLY: Your non-dominant hand is in the 1 handshape held in front of the body, palm to the side. The dominant hand is in the V handshape, with the palm facing the side. Begin the sign with the V hand vertical, and then bring the hand down so that the V fingers go around the 1 finger and end with the palm facing down. This is the sign to use for "apply to," "application," "applicable," or "to file."

2ND: Hold your 2 hand in front of your body with your palm starting to the side. Twist your wrist quickly, ending with your palm facing in.

FLOOR: Both hands are in the B handshape. Hold them together in front of your body with the palms facing down. Move your hands apart from each other to show the floor. To indicate multiple floors (in a building with two or more), draw the first floor; then move your hand up a few inches and sign FLOOR again.

PAYCHECK: This is a combination sign of PAY and then showing the shape of a check. First sign PAY with your non-dominant hand in the open B handshape and your dominant hand in the 1 handshape, fingertip in the middle of your non-dominant hand's palm. Flick the finger forward and off the palm. Then move both hands to the bent L handshapes. They begin together with the index fingers and thumbs touching, then move your hands out to show the edges of a check, and then pinch each index finger and thumb together to show the short edges of the check.

DEPARTMENT: This is very similar to FAMILY. You will sign it the same way, but with the D handshapes. Both hands are in the D handshape, starting in front of your body, with the D hands together and palm facing out. Trace a circle with your hands ending with the Ds together on the pinky side, with the palms facing in.

MEETING: Your hands are in a modified 5 handshape. Bring your hands together in front of you with the thumbs touching and the remaining fingers pointed up. Bring the fingertips together to meet above your thumbs. Tap them together twice. This is for a gathering of people, not to meet someone.

OFFICE: Both hands are in the O handshape, with your hands horizontal and palms facing in. Hold your dominant hand in front of your non-dominant hand. Bend your wrists so your palms are now facing each other.

PHONE CALL: Your non-dominant hand is in the flat B handshape, with the palm facing down. Your dominant hand is in the open B handshape, with the palm facing down. Your dominant hand starts just above the back of the dominant hand, drops down on top of the hand and then pull the fingers off and back. As you pull, bend the dominant hand fingers into a loose open A handshape.

EXERCISE 6.1 WORD BANK

Pair each sign with the correct word. When you're finished, practice each of the word bank signs in the mirror.

PAYCHECK	JOB	MEETING	SECOND
PRINTER	WORK	OFFICE	FLOOR
DEPARTMENT	APPLY		

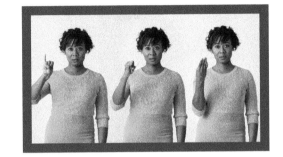

1. ....

2. ....

3. ....

4. ....

5. ....

6. ....

7. ....

8. ....

6.2 Office Culture

In this lesson, you'll learn how to communicate regarding common occurrences with colleagues and in work environments.

I sent you an email.

EMAIL

I

SEND-you

I'll give you the USB that has the saved file.

FILE

I

SAVE

USB

GIVE-you

We have a team event.

TEAM

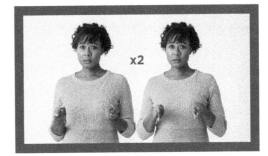

HAPPEN

WE

HAVE

RELATED VOCABULARY

FORWARD

BOSS

TECHNOLOGY

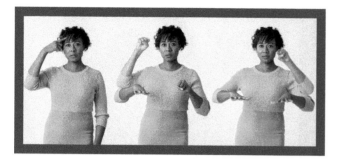

BRAINSTORM

RESPONSIBLE

EMAIL: Your non-dominant hand is in the flat C handshape, with the palm facing to the side. Your dominant hand is in the 1 handshape. Start with the dominant hand's finger pointing toward your body; then swipe it forward in the open space of the C hand so that the finger ends pointing at a forward angle.

SEND (electronically): Your dominant hand starts in the baby O handshape, with the palm facing down. Flick your index finger out and slightly move your hand forward as you do.

FILE: Both hands are in the open B handshape. The non-dominant hand is vertical, with the palm facing the side. The dominant hand is horizontal, with the palm facing in. Slide the dominant hand between the middle and ring fingers of the non-dominant hand.

USB: Fingerspell USB.

SAVE: The non-dominant hand is in the S handshape held near the chest. The dominant hand is in the V handshape. Tap the back of your S hand with your V hand twice.

GIVE-to: Your dominant hand is in the X handshape. Move the hand from in front of yourself forward toward the person you are signing to.

TEAM: You sign TEAM the same way you do FAMILY and DEPARTMENT, but with the T handshape. Both hands are in the T handshape, starting in front of your body with the T hands together, with the palm facing out. Trace a circle with your hands ending with the Ts together on the pinky side, with the palms facing in.

EVENT: This is the same sign as HAPPEN. Both hands are in the 1 handshape, held horizontally in front of the body with the palms facing each other. Twist your wrists to bring the hands down, with the palms facing down. Repeat this movement twice.

FORWARD: Hold your dominant hand in the F handshape with the palm facing down. Move the hand forward in a small arch.

BOSS: Your dominant hand is in the bent 5 handshape. Tap your dominant shoulder twice with your hand on top of the shoulder.

TECHNOLOGY: Your non-dominant hand is held vertically, with the palm facing to the side, in the open B handshape. The dominant hand is in the modified 5 handshape with the middle finger extended forward. Tap the side of your palm with the tip of your middle finger twice.

BRAINSTORM: First sign THINK with your dominant hand in the 1 handshape and tap the side of your forehead. Then move both hands into loose O handshapes, with the palms facing down, and open the hands into loose 5 handshapes. You open the hands in an alternating motion, and as you do, you move the hands in a downward motion. This is signing THINK plus plopping a bunch of ideas down onto paper.

RESPONSIBLE: Both hands are in the bent B handshape and you tap the front of your dominant shoulder twice.

AN ONGOING FIGHT FOR JUSTICE

People who are Deaf or Hard of Hearing have a constant battle for equal access to—and fair treatment within—education, employment, legal institutions, and basic services such as medical care. Many Deaf children are not taught sign language or are left with limited means to communicate. These kids often do not have access to adequate curriculum, captioning, and interpreters; many are expected to learn by lip-reading alone. Even with supportive education, the unemployment rate in the Deaf community is very high since employers are not required to educate themselves on how to understand, support, communicate, and integrate Deaf and HoH people onto the team. Many times, they'll overlook a qualified Deaf candidate for someone far less qualified but hearing.

The interactions between the Deaf and law enforcement can be dangerous. Signing is often misconstrued as a threat, or people are considered "non-compliant" because they do not hear orders. These misunderstandings can be fatal. Later, members of the Deaf community are not provided with interpreters, leading to false imprisonment, unfair trials, and coerced confessions. Deaf people are also often left without a qualified interpreter in critical medical situations: Writing notes back and forth with your doctor is not okay. If you're hearing, it's important to learn more about what you can do to support the Deaf community in medical and legal scenarios.

EXERCISE 6.2 MULTIPLE CHOICE

Choose the correct sign to match each word.

1. BOSS

A.

B.

C.

2. RESPONSIBLE

A.

B.

C.

3. EMAIL

A.

B.

C.

4. TECHNOLOGY

A.

B.

C.

6.3 Technology

In this lesson, you'll learn many technology signs and how to communicate your tech needs.

The internet is down.

INTERNET

INTERNET-DOWN

I spilled coffee on my laptop.

MY

LAPTOP

COFFEE

I

SPILL-CUP

Click the link to install the program.

PROGRAM

INSTALL

HOW?

LINK

CLICK

RELATED VOCABULARY

COMPUTER

LAPTOP

SYSTEM

DOWNLOAD

MOUSE

INTERNET: Both hands are in the modified 5 handshape, with the middle fingers extended forward. Touch the fingertips of the middle fingers together in front of your body and twist the dominant hand slightly side to side.

INTERNET-DOWN: You first begin by signing INTERNET; then you drop your dominant hand forward so that it's lying horizontally.

COFFEE: Both hands are in the S handshape, with the palms facing the side, and your dominant hand on top. Move your dominant hand in a counterclockwise circle twice. This sign represents grinding coffee.

SPILL-CUP: You begin this sign with your dominant hand in the C handshape. Tip your hand forward, as if you were spilling your cup. In this sentence, you are spilling coffee on your laptop, so you'll need to spill it in the direction of where you signed LAPTOP. As you tilt your hand toward your laptop, both hands form the flat O handshape. With your hands close together, move both hands forward into the 5 handshapes to mimic the liquid spilling over the laptop.

PROGRAM: Your non-dominant hand is in the open B handshape, with the palm facing in and vertical. The dominant hand is in the P handshape.

Place the P on the palm of the non-dominant hand and slide it up, over, and down the backside of the hand.

INSTALL: Both hands are in the V handshape, up near the shoulders, palms facing each other. The dominant hand is just above the non-dominant hand. Drag the hands down, and as you reach the bottom of the movement, bend the wrists so that the hands are now horizontal. As you do this, they change into the bent V handshape.

LINK: Both hands are in the open F handshape, with the palms facing down. Bring the hands together and as the index finger and thumbs come together, circle them both into the F handshape to form a link between the two hands.

CLICK: Your dominant hand is in the modified 5 handshape, with the middle finger extended forward. Hold your hand up in front of your body with the palm out. Tap the space in front of you with your middle finger.

COMPUTER: Your non-dominant arm is held in front of your body, and your dominant hand is in the C handshape. Move your C hand up your arm by tapping in an upward arching motion two to three times.

LAPTOP: Both hands are in the flat B handshape. Start with both hands together, your dominant hand with the palm facing down and the non-dominant hand with the palm facing up. Open up your dominant hand twice. This is mimicking the opening of a laptop.

SYSTEM: Both hands are in the Y handshape, with the palms facing down and thumbs touching. Move your hands apart a few inches and then straight down.

DOWNLOAD: Both hands are in the 4 handshape with the palms facing each other. Start with the hands up near the head, the dominant hand higher than the non-dominant hand. Bring the hands down, and as you do, bend the wrists so that the hands end the movement in the horizontal position.

MOUSE: Your dominant hand is in the bent 3 handshape with the palm facing down. Hold it in front of your body and circle the hand in a clockwise motion twice.

EXERCISE 6.3 FILL IN

Identify each sign. Write the answer in the space provided below each image.

1. _____

2. _____

3. _____

4. _____

5. _____

CHAPTER 6 PROGRESS CHECK

Match each sign with the correct word.

COMPUTER	POLICE OFFICER	WORK	LAWYER
LAPTOP	BOSS	MEETING	COFFEE
INSTALL	EMAIL	PAYCHECK	FUTURE
PROGRAM	TEAM	APPLY	DOWNLOAD
MANAGER	APPLY	EVENT	CLICK
ENGINEER	CAREER	WIFI	

1. ....

2. ....

3. ....

4. ....

5. ....

6. ....

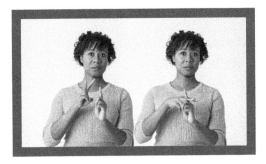

7. ....

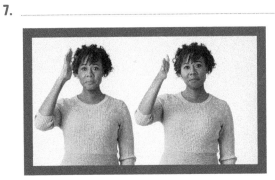

8. ....

9. ....

NAVIGATING THE EARTH

In this chapter, you'll learn how to identify basic geography and navigation, various natural elements, and everyday weather patterns. Specifically, you'll find:

- Basic geography
- Seasons and weather
- Navigation

7.1 Basic Geography

In this lesson, you'll learn how to sign the seven continents and a few US states.

I grew up in Texas.

TEXAS

I

GREW-UP

I'm flying to New York in the morning.

TOMORROW

MORNING

NEW YORK

I

FLY

Are you going to Disneyland in California or Disney World in Florida?

DISNEY

CALIFORNIA

DISNEY

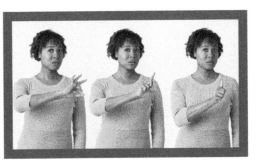

FLORIDA

GO

WHICH?

RELATED VOCABULARY

AFRICA

AUSTRALIA

EUROPE

ASIA

NORTH AMERICA

SOUTH AMERICA

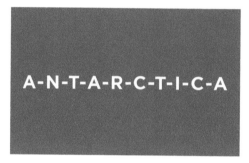

A-N-T-A-R-C-T-I-C-A

ANTARCTICA

TEXAS: With your dominant hand in the X hand-shape, palm out, draw a short horizontal line with your hand forward your side and then change direction and draw a short vertical line down.

GROW-UP: Your dominant hand is in the open B handshape with the palm facing down. Start with your hand at waist height and pull your hand up to about eye level. This is as if your hand was on top of a child's head and stayed there as they grew taller and taller.

NEW YORK: Your non-dominant hand is in the open B handshape, with the palm facing up, and your dominant hand is in the Y handshape, with the palm facing down. Place the Y hand on top of the B hand and move it back and forth across the palm.

DISNEY: Place both hands in the bent 5 hand-shape on top of your head to show the ears of Mickey Mouse.

CALIFORNIA: Your dominant hand is in the L-I handshape, with the palm facing the side. Place your index finger on your check and pull your hand down. As you do, drop your index finger so that your hand is now in the Y handshape.

FLORIDA: You will fingerspell the letters F-L-A, but as you do, make an arch with your hand: F as the bottom of the arch, L as the high middle, and A as the end of the arch.

AFRICA: Your dominant hand is in the flat O hand-shape with the palm facing out and in front of your body. You will trace the shape of Africa by opening your hand from the flat O shape into a wide C, and close your hand back into the flat O handshape as you reach the tip of the continent. This entire sign is done in a smooth, fluid motion.

AUSTRALIA: Hold both hands in the 8 handshape, with the palms facing down. In an upward arch, bring your hands up and forward and end the arch by opening your hands out into the 5 handshape.

EUROPE: Your dominant hand is in the E hand-shape, with the palm facing the side. Draw a circle with the E near the side of your forehead.

ASIA: Your dominant hand starts in the A hand-shape, with the palm facing out. Move the hand in a circle, starting in a downward circle out toward the side. As your hand starts the upward motion of the circle, open your hand into the 5 handshape and end above where your A hand started.

NORTH AMERICA: This is a combination sign of NORTH and AMERICA. Sign NORTH by holding your dominant hand in the N handshape, with the palm facing out, and move the hand straight up a few inches. Sign AMERICAN with both hands in the 5 handshape, fingers interlaced with the palms facing in and the fingertips of both hands pointing out. Move the interlaced hands in a counterclockwise circle.

SOUTH AMERICA: This is a combination sign of SOUTH and AMERICA. Sign SOUTH by holding your dominant hand in the S handshape, with the palm facing out, and move the hand straight down a few inches. Sign AMERICA with both hands in the 5 handshape fingers interlaced with the palms facing in and the fingertips of both hands pointing out. Move the interlaced hands in a counterclockwise circle.

ANTARCTICA: This is fingerspelled.

THE 50 UNITED STATES

Several states have their own sign, but many use their postal code as their state sign. It would be cumbersome to include all 50 state signs in this workbook, so I encourage you to fingerspell the postal codes for each state until you are able to learn the signs later. Ask people in your local Deaf community for signs related to your state. For instance, you can ask them the signs for your state, the cities and communities around you, and any other local landmarks.

EXERCISE 7.1 WORD BANK

Pair each sign with the correct word. When you're finished, practice each of the word bank signs in the mirror.

AFRICA	ASIA	SOUTH AMERICA	NEW YORK
AUSTRALIA	EUROPE	TEXAS	GROW-UP
	NORTH AMERICA	CALIFORNIA	

1. _____

2. _____

3. _____

4. _____

5. _____

6. _____

7. _____

8. _____

9. _____

10. _____

7.2 Seasons and Weather

In this lesson, you'll gain a basic ability to communicate through the seasons and chat about their associated weather patterns.

Summer is my favorite time of the year.

MY

FAVORITE

SEASON

WHAT?

SUMMER

It's pouring outside.

NOW

RAIN++

Did you see the snow?

SNOW

YOU

PHRASE CONTINUES>

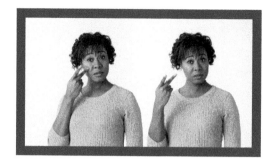

SEE?

RELATED VOCABULARY

FALL

WINTER

SPRING

CLOUDS

WIND

FAVORITE: This is the same sign as PREFER. Your dominant hand is in the 5 handshape with the middle finger extended forward. Tap your chin with the tip of your middle finger.

SEASON: Your non-dominant hand is in the open B handshape, with the palm facing the side. Your dominant hand is in the S handshape, with the palm facing out. Place the S on the palm of your other hand and circle your hand on the palm once.

SUMMER: Your dominant hand starts in the 1 handshape, with the palm facing down, held in front your forehead. Pull your hand across your forehead, and change into the X handshape as you pull it across.

RAIN: Both hands are in the 5 handshape, with the palms facing out. Bend your wrist and bring your hands down so that your hands are lower and your palms are facing down. Repeat this motion one more time.

SNOW: Hold both of your 5 hands up in the air, near your head. Flutter your fingers as you move your hands down and side to side.

SEE: Your dominant hand is in the 2 handshape, with the palm facing in. Place the tip of the middle finger underneath the eye and move your hand forward.

FALL: Your non-dominant arm is bent, with the hand held up by your shoulder. Your dominant hand is in the flat B handshape with the side of the index finger resting on the elbow. Brush your elbow twice in a downward motion.

WINTER: Both hands are in the W handshape, with the palms facing in, and shake your hands side to side.

SPRING: Your non-dominant hand is in the flat C handshape, with the palm facing the side. Your dominant hand is in the flat O handshape, with the palm facing up. Place the fingertips of the flat O hand in the space between the flat C hand. Push your hand up through the opening, and as you do, open the hand into a 5 hand that is in a cone shape. Repeat this motion one more time. This is showing a plant growing out of the ground.

CLOUD: Both hands are in the bent 5 handshape, hands up above your head with your non-dominant hand slightly lower than your dominant hand. Your non-dominant hand is facing palm out, and your dominant hand is palm in. Make alternating circles in the air with both hands.

WIND: Both hands are in the 5 handshape, with the palms facing each other. Move the arms from the elbow, side to side.

EXERCISE 7.2 MULTIPLE CHOICE

Choose the correct sign to match each word.

1. FAVORITE

2. RAIN

3. CLOUD

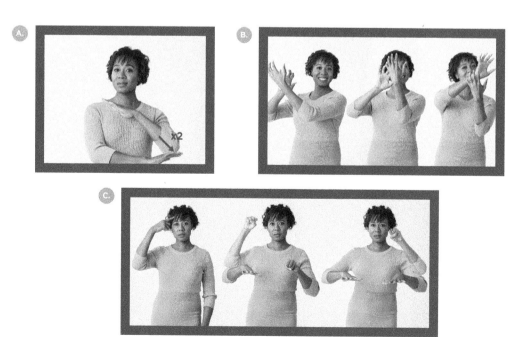

7.3 Navigation

In this lesson, you'll be able to communicate directions with others.

The river is to the north.

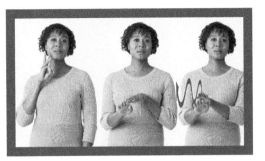

RIVER

THERE

NORTH

The birds are flying south for the winter.

BIRD

WINTER

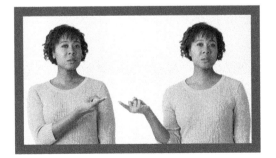

THEY

FLY

PHRASE CONTINUES>

SOUTH

Do you prefer the city or the country?

CITY

COUNTRY

YOU

PREFER

WHICH?

RELATED VOCABULARY

WORLD

CONTINENTS

EAST

WEST

LEFT

RIGHT

RIVER: This is a combination sign of WATER and WAVES. First sign WATER with the W hand tapping the chin and then moving into signing WAVES with both hands in the flat B handshape, with the palms facing down. Your hands are held out with your dominant hand in front and your non-dominant hand behind. Move your hands up and down in a rolling motion, showing the up and down of waves.

NORTH: Hold your dominant hand in the N hand-shape, with the palm facing out, and move the hand straight up a few inches.

BIRD: Your dominant hand is in the G handshape, held against the side of the cheek with the fingers

near the mouth. Pinch your index finger and thumb together twice.

THEY: This is the same sign as YOU-all. With your dominant hand in the 1 handshape, start with the hand pointing across your body to the non-dominant side. Sweep your hand in front of your body. You can sign this generally, or if you are referring to a specific group of people, begin the sign in front of the first person and end the sweep at the last person.

SOUTH: Hold your dominant hand in the S hand-shape, with the palm facing out, and move the hand straight down a few inches.

CITY: Both hands are in the open B handshape, with the palms facing each other and fingertips together. Twist your hands in.

COUNTRY: Hold your non-dominant arm up with your hand near your shoulder. Your dominant hand is in the open B handshape, placed on the elbow. Move your hand in a circle two times on the elbow.

WORLD: Both hands are in the W handshape, with the palms facing the side. Your non-dominant hand is down and your dominant hand is on top. Circle your dominant hand around the non-dominant hand, landing back on top of the non-dominant hand.

CONTINENT: Your non-dominant hand is in the bent 5 handshape, held in front of the body, with the palm facing down. Your dominant hand is in a C handshape with the fingers spread out, as if holding a baseball. Tap the fingertips of your loose C hand in two or three random spots on your non-dominant hand. Your non-dominant hand represents the globe, and your dominant hand is showing a few land masses around the globe.

EAST: Hold your dominant hand up in the E handshape and move it toward the right.

WEST: Hold your dominant hand up in the W handshape and move it toward the right.

LEFT: Hold your dominant hand up in the L handshape and move it toward your left.

RIGHT: Hold your dominant hand up in the R handshape and move it toward your right.

GRAMMAR TIP: USING THE SPACE AROUND YOU

ASL isn't a linear language—it's a complex visual-spatial language. When you sign, you use the space around you to show the story. You can place people and objects around you to show their location and relationship relative to one another. You can add in classifiers to show what's happening to these objects or people. You can shift your body in different angles to show various characters in a story.

As a beginning signer, start to use the space around you by signing the name of an object and pointing to where it is before naming another object and pointing to where it is in relationship to the first. For example, sign RIVER and then point to your left; then sign BIRD and point to show the location of the bird relative to the river. You can add in other objects, animals, or people and where they are as well. Think of the space around you as a 3-dimensional map and use it to show what's happening.

EXERCISE 7.3 WORD BANK

Pair each sign with the correct word. When you're finished, practice each of the word bank signs in the mirror.

RIVER	SOUTH	WORLD	WEST
NORTH	CITY	CONTINENTS	LEFT
BIRD	COUNTRY	EAST	RIGHT

1. _____

2. _____

3. _____

4. _____

5. _____

6. _____

7. _____

8. _____

9. _____

10. _____

CHAPTER 7 PROGRESS CHECK

Identify each sign. Write the answer in the space provided below each image.

1. ....

2. ....

3. ....

4. ....

5. ....

6. ....

8

TRAVEL

In this chapter, you will gain a basic sense of how to get from point A to point B and communicate your transportation needs. You'll learn things like:

- Getting from A to B

- Planes, trains, and automobiles

- Vacations

8.1 Getting from A to B

In this lesson, you'll learn to discuss how to move from one location to another and ask for directions.

How do I get to ___?

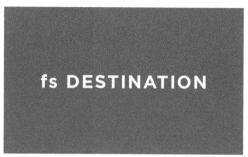

fs DESTINATION

ARRIVE

HOW?

What time do you leave?

YOU

LEAVE

TIME?

TICKET

YOU

BUY?

RELATED VOCABULARY

GET IN

RIDE IN/ON

GET OUT

INTERSECTION

CORNER

ARRIVE: Both hands are in the open B handshape. Hold your non-dominant hand out, with the palm facing up. Your dominant hand starts with the palm facing in and arches forward and down slowly, landing on the non-dominant palm.

TICKET: Your non-dominant hand is in the open B handshape, with the palm facing up, and your dominant hand is in the bent 2 handshape, with the palm facing in. Move your dominant hand toward your non-dominant hand, sandwiching the edge of your non-dominant hand between the index and middle fingers of your dominant hand.

LEAVE: Your dominant hand begins in the 5 handshape, with the palm to the side, and held up above your shoulder. Pull your hand out, away from your body, toward the side, closing into the flat O handshape.

TIME (what time): You sign TIME, with your non-dominant hand in the S handshape. Your dominant hand is in the 1 handshape, with a slight bend. Tap your finger on your wrist once, where your watch would be. When you're asking the question "What time?" tap your wrist twice, with a slight pause after your second tap. To make it a question, furrow your eyebrows and tilt your head forward.

GET IN: Your non-dominant hand is in the C handshape, with the palm facing the side. Your dominant hand is in the bent 2 handshape, with the palm facing the side. Bring your hand down and

twist your wrist to hook your dominant hand fingers over the thumb of your non-dominant hand. This shows the legs sitting (the bent 2) on the seat (the thumb of the C).

RIDE IN/ON: Your non-dominant hand is in the C handshape, with the palm facing to the side. Your dominant hand is in the bent 2 handshape, with the palm facing down. Hook your bent 2 fingers on the thumb of the C hand. Pull your C hand forward, moving the bent 2 hand with it.

GET OUT: Your non-dominant hand is in the C handshape, with the palm facing to the side. Your dominant hand is in the bent 2 handshape, with the palm facing down. Start with your bent 2 fingers hooked on the thumb of the C hand. Then jut the fingers out and off the thumb to the side.

INTERSECTION: Both hands are in the 1 handshape, hands held horizontally. The palm of your non-dominant hand is facing in, and the palm of your dominant hand is facing the side. Tap the middle of your dominant hand's finger on top of the middle of your non-dominant hand's finger two times. Your fingers will be in the shape of a lowercase T.

CORNER: Both hands are in the flat B handshape and horizontal. Bring the fingertips of both hands together to form a right angle, or corner, with your hands.

EXERCISE 8.1 FILL IN

Identify each sign. Write the answer in the space provided below each image.

1. ....

2. ....

3. ....

4. ....

5. ....

6. ....

8.2 Planes, Trains, and Automobiles

In this lesson, you'll learn to discuss various methods of transportation and how to get around.

Are you taking the train?

TRAIN

YOU

RIDE-IN?

What time does your flight arrive?

YOUR

PLANE

ARRIVE

TIME?

Can I order you a taxi?

TAXI

NEED?

I

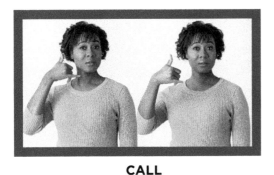

CALL

CAN

RELATED VOCABULARY

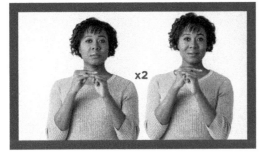

SUBWAY

BACK-AND-FORTH

TRANSFER

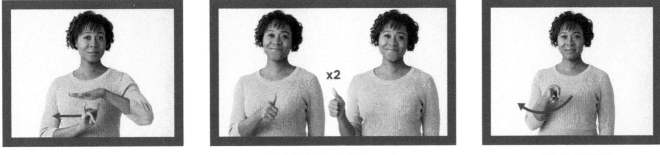

HIGHWAY

TRAFFIC

TRAIN: Both hands are in the H handshape, with the palms facing down. Place the dominant hand fingers on top of the non-dominant hand's fingers, with the fingertips pointing in opposite directions. Rub your dominant hand along the top of the fingers back and forth.

TAXI: Fingerspell the word, T-A-X-I.

CAN: Both hands are in the A handshape, arms held out in front of you, and parallel to the floor. Your wrists are bent up so that your palms are facing out. Bring the palms down in a sharp movement with your mouth in a firm line.

CALL (summon): Your non-dominant hand is in the flat B handshape, with the palm facing down. Your dominant hand is in the open B handshape, with the palm facing down. Your dominant hand starts just above the back of the non-dominant hand. Drop down on top of the hand and then pull the fingers off and back. As you pull, bend the dominant hand fingers into a loose open A handshape.

SUBWAY: Your non-dominant hand is in the flat B handshape, with the palm facing down. Your dominant hand is in the Y handshape, with the palm facing out. Your Y hand is underneath the B hand, with the tops of your knuckles touching the palm. Move the hand forward and backward twice.

BACK-AND-FORTH: Your dominant hand is in the open A handshape, in the thumbs-up position, with the palm to the side. Move your hand in, out, and then back in.

TRANSFER: Your dominant hand is in the bent 2 handshape, with the palm facing down. Bend your wrist to the side in order to swing your hand out.

HIGHWAY: Both hands are in the N handshape, with the palms facing each other. Move both hands past each other two times.

TRAFFIC: Both hands are in the 5 handshape, with the palms facing down and the dominant hand in front of the non-dominant hand. Bring your hands forward in two quick stop-and-go movements.

ADVENTURING WHILE DEAF OR HOH

Here are some things to consider if you or someone you know is Deaf or Hard of Hearing and traveling:

- Carry a card that identifies your hearing status. Show this to people and communicate with those at the airport, hotel, train, bus, tour group, restaurants, and so on that you are Deaf or Hard of Hearing.

- Be careful when around border agents or police, as pulling out a card from your pocket might be perceived as hostile. Slowly and carefully sign that you are Deaf and gesture, asking if they can write for you.

- Before you travel to a new country, take the time to look up which hand gestures are offensive in their country. Pointing, the thumbs up, signing OKAY, and the five handshapes can be seen as rude in some countries.

- Carry on your hearing aids, CIs, and batteries rather than check them.

- Inform your flight attendants and seatmates of your hearing status so they can alert you of any possible emergencies, announcements, or turbulence.

- Use your smartphone to communicate.

- Do your research and be prepared so that you can enjoy your trip to its fullest.

EXERCISE 8.2 MULTIPLE CHOICE

Choose the correct sign to match each word.

1. SUBWAY

2. TRANSFER

3. TRAIN

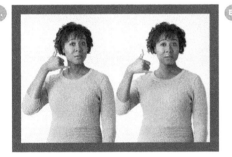

4. HIGHWAY

8.3 Vacations

In this lesson, you'll learn to talk about your vacations, holidays, and getaways.

I'm going to Hawaii with my friends for spring break.

SPRING

BREAK

WITH

MY

FRIENDS

GO

HAWAII

Last week I flew to Canada.

PAST WEEK

CANADA

I

FLY

Are you driving to _____?

fs LOCATION

YOU

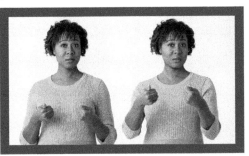

DRIVE?

RELATED VOCABULARY

HOTEL

RENTAL

TRAVEL

HONEYMOON

VACATION

BREAK: Your non-dominant hand is in the flat B handshape, with the palm facing to the side. Your dominant hand is in the flat B handshape, with the palm facing down. Slide the dominant hand between the middle and ring fingers of the non-dominant hand.

FRIEND: Both hands are in the X handshape. Your non-dominant hand is facing palm up and your dominant hand is facing palm down. Hook the index fingers together in this position and then flip the hands so that the dominant hand is now on the bottom and the non-dominant hand is on top.

HAWAII: Your dominant hand is in the H handshape, with the palm facing in. Draw a circle around your face with your H hand.

CANADA: Your dominant hand is in the A handshape, with the palm facing in. Tap your dominant side chest twice with two small taps, with your hand held horizontally.

HOTEL: Your non-dominant hand is in the 1 handshape, palm facing the side, hand vertical. Your dominant hand is in the H handshape, with the palm facing in. Place the H hand on the tip of the index finger and tap the air toward your body with the H fingers.

RENTAL: Both hands are in the 1 handshape. Your non-dominant hand is vertical, with the palm facing out. The dominant hand is horizontal, with the palm facing you. In a downward movement, drag the dominant hand down the non-dominant hand 3 times. This is the sign for MONTH, but the movement is done three times. Use this sign no matter the length of the time of the rental.

TRAVEL: Your dominant hand is in the bent 2 handshape, with the palm facing down. Move your hand out and away from yourself in a counter-clockwise circle.

HONEYMOON: Your dominant hand is in the modified 5 handshape with the middle finger extended forward. Draw a short line down your chin with the tip of your middle finger on the dominant hand side, and then another on the non-dominant hand side.

VACATION: Both hands are in the 5 handshape. Tap the thumbs onto your chest, a few inches from your armpits, two times.

EXERCISE 8.3 WORD BANK

Pair each sign with the correct word. When you're finished, practice each of the word bank signs in the mirror.

SPRING	HAWAII	RENTAL	MUSEUM
BREAK	CANADA	CRUISE	WITH
FRIEND	HOTEL	ISLAND	GO

1. _____

2. _____

3. _____

4. _____

5. _____

6. _____

CHAPTER 8 PROGRESS CHECK

Choose the correct sign to match each word.

1. ARRIVE

A. 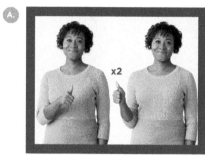   B.    C.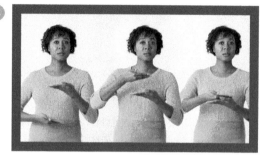

2. SUBWAY

A.    B.    C.

3. HOTEL

A.    B.    C.

4. TRAVEL

A.    B.    C.

9

RELIGION AND HOLIDAYS

In this chapter, you'll get a basic foundation for discussing global religions, holidays, and celebrations. You'll learn things like:

- World religion basics
- Major US holidays
- Passover, Easter, and Ramadan
- Feasts and holiday celebrations

9.1 Global Religions

In this lesson, you'll get a basic introduction to the religions found around the world and in the United States.

As-salaamu Alaikum! Ramadan Mubarak.

AS-SALAAMU ALAIKUM

HAPPY

RAMADAN

I will go to church on Christmas.

CHRISTMAS

CHURCH

I

GO

I know her from temple.

SHE

I

MEET

WHERE?

TEMPLE

RELATED VOCABULARY

JEWISH/JUDAISM

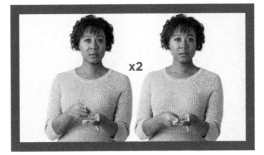

BUDDHISM

HINDU

ISLAM/ISLAMIC

CHRISTIAN

AGNOSTIC

AS-SALAAMU ALAIKUM: This is an Islamic sign that means "Peace be upon you." Your dominant hand starts out in the open B handshape at the side of the head. Place the side of the index finger to the side of the forehead; then bring your hand up and out as if saluting. Immediately drop your hand down to your side into the open A handshape, and move it up and down a few inches.

RAMADAN (fasting): Your dominant hand is in the F handshape. Place the circled index finger and thumb on the corner of your mouth, on the non-dominant side, and slide it across your lips to end at the opposite corner of your mouth.

CHRISTMAS: Your dominant hand is in the C handshape, with the palm facing out. Start with the hand up near the head on your non-dominant side. Arch your hand across your body, ending on the dominant side. Your wrist twists as you arch your hand so that at the end of the arch, your palm is facing in.

CHURCH: Your non-dominant hand is in the S handshape, with the palm facing down. Your dominant hand is in the C handshape, with the palm facing out. Tap the thumb of your C hand on the back of your S hand twice.

TEMPLE: Your non-dominant hand is in the S handshape, with the palm facing down. Your dominant hand is in the T handshape, with the palm facing out. Tap the base of your T hand on the back of your S hand twice.

JEWISH/JUDAISM: Your dominant hand starts in the 4 handshape, with the palm facing in. Place the fingertips on the chin, with your thumb underneath your chin. Pull your hand down into the flat O handshape. Do this motion twice. It's important that your palm is facing your body, and not to the side.

BUDDHISM: Your non-dominant hand is in the 7-8 handshape. This means both your middle and ring fingers are touching your thumb, and your pinky and index fingers are extended. Hold your non-dominant hand down horizontally with the palm facing the side. Your dominant hand is in the 1 handshape, horizontal and palm facing the side. With your dominant hand, tap the circled fingers of your non-dominant hand twice.

HINDU: There are two variations for this sign. The most common is to sign HINDU with your dominant hand in the 1 handshape: Place the tip of the finger, palm in, at the center of your forehead, just above your eyebrows and twist. The second variation is to do this same sign as above; then bring both hands together in the prayer position, both hands in the flat B handshape, palms together in front of your chest.

ISLAM/ISLAMIC: Your dominant hand is in the baby C handshape. Hold your hand out, with the palm facing out, and shake your C hand.

CHRISTIAN: This is a combination of CHRIST and PERSON. Your dominant hand is in the C handshape. Place your hand on your non-dominant shoulder; then bring your hand down to touch at your waist on the dominant side. Then sign PERSON with both hands in the open B handshape, with the palms facing each other, and bring your hands down.

AGNOSTIC: This is a combination sign of DOUBT and GOD. Your dominant hand first signs DOUBT with the hand in the 2 handshape, with the palm facing in and in front of the eyes. Bend the fingers twice. Then sign GOD with your dominant hand in the flat B handshape, with the palm to the side. Start with your hand above your head on your dominant side and hand horizontal. Bring the fingertips of your hand up in a semicircle, ending with your hand vertical.

EXERCISE 9.1 MULTIPLE CHOICE

Choose the correct sign to match each word.

1. RAMADAN

A.

B.

C.

2. CHURCH

A.

B.

C.

3. JEWISH

A.

B.

C.

4. BUDDHISM

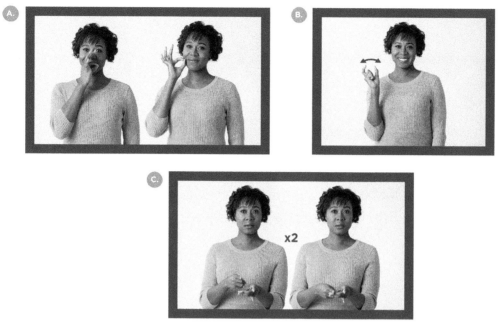

5. HINDU

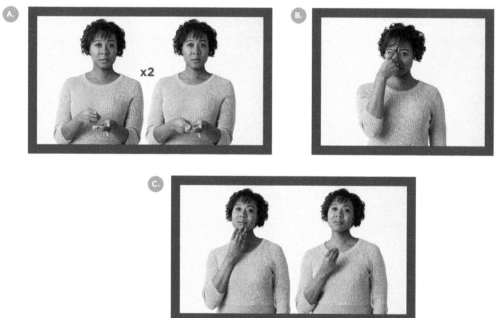

9.2 Holidays

In this lesson, you'll learn the signs for some familiar holidays celebrated in the United States.

What are you doing on Valentine's Day?

VALENTINE'S DAY

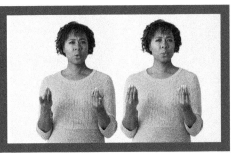

YOU

WHAT-DO?

I love to watch the parades on Independence Day.

INDEPENDENCE DAY

PARADES

I

WATCH

KISS-FIST

What's your favorite food on Thanksgiving?

THANKSGIVING DAY

YOUR

FAVORITE

PHRASE CONTINUES>

FOOD

WHAT?

RELATED VOCABULARY

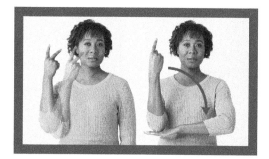

MEMORIAL DAY

ST. PATRICK'S DAY

NEW YEAR

HALLOWEEN

VETERANS DAY

VALENTINE'S DAY: Both hands are in the modified 5 handshape with the middle fingers extended forward. With the tips of your middle fingers, place them over your heart on your chest and draw a heart with both hands. Then sign DAY.

WHAT-DO: Both hands are in the D handshape, with the palms facing up. Tap your index finger on your thumb two to three times. While you sign this your eyebrows are furrowed and your mouth is in the "ooo" shape, as if you were saying "do."

INDEPENDENCE DAY: Both of your hands are in the I handshape, arms crossed over each other with the palms facing in. Uncross your arms, ending with your hands up by your shoulders, with the palms facing out. Next, sign DAY. You can also sign this by fingerspelling J-U-L-Y and 4th. You sign 4th with your 4 hand, held out with the palm facing down and twisting toward your body.

PARADE: Both hands are in the 5 handshape, with the palms facing down and fingertips extended toward the floor. Your dominant hand is in front of your non-dominant hand. Bend the wrists forward, backward, and forward again in a quick motion. This is simulating the many legs walking in the parade.

KISS-FIST: Your dominant hand is in the S handshape, with the palm facing out. Place the back of your S hand on your lips and push the hand out in a quick movement. As you do this, you kiss the back of your hand. It's important that your facial expressions look emphatic about your love for the subject of your sentence. It's a firm, determined look.

THANKSGIVING: Both hands are in the open B handshape, with the palms facing in. Place the fingertips of your dominant hand on your chin and have your non-dominant hand in the same position, but in the air below and to the side of your chin. You are signing THANK-YOU with both hands, in a double arch. Bring the hands down and then arch the hands up and forward one more time. This is a quick double movement.

MEMORIAL DAY: This is a combination of LOOK-BACK and DAY. First sign LOOK-BACK with your dominant hand in the 2 handshape, with the palm facing in. Place the tip of the middle finger underneath your eye. Then arch your hand to the side and back. Next, sign DAY.

ST. PATRICK'S DAY: Your dominant hand is in the X handshape. Place the crook of your X into the bicep of your non-dominant arm and twist it once, as if turning a key in a lock. Then sign DAY.

NEW YEAR: This is a combination sign of NEW and YEAR. The non-dominant hand is in the open B handshape, and the dominant hand is in the bent B handshape. Using your dominant hand, make a scooping motion on the palm of your non-dominant hand, leading with the fingertips and going in the direction of the length of your non-dominant hand. Then sign YEAR with both hands in the S handshape. Place the dominant hand on top of the non-dominant hand, with both hands held horizontally. Circle the dominant hand around the non-dominant hand, landing back on top of the non-dominant hand.

HALLOWEEN: Both hands are in the flat B handshape, with the palms facing in, and held in front of your eyes. Pull your hands out away from your eyes to the sides of your head. Do this motion twice. It's like you're playing peek-a-boo.

VETERANS DAY: Fingerspell V-E-T and then sign DAY.

KISS-FIST

KISS-FIST is an ASL idiom, or figure of speech, that means "I *love* it." This isn't to be used as a way of declaring your love for a person (it does not mean "I love you"), but, rather, it is a declaration of deep liking of a subject or object. For instance, if you're obsessed with a book series you just read, you'd say you KISS-FIST it. A travel destination you fell in love with you would KISS-FIST as well. You would not KISS-FIST your sister, no matter how much you love her.

EXERCISE 9.2 WORD BANK

Pair each sign with the correct word. When you're finished, practice each of the word bank signs in the mirror.

1. ....

2. ....

3. ....

4. ....

5. ....

6. ....

7. ....

9.3 Meals and Celebrations

Here you'll find the basics for various celebrations and parties associated with the world religions you've just learned to sign.

My whole family is celebrating ___ with a feast.

MY

FULL

FAMILY

WE

CELEBRATE

fs THE HOLIDAY

HOW?

FEAST

My godson is getting baptized soon.

MY

GODSON

SOON

PHRASE CONTINUES>

HE

BAPTIZED

His rabbi is meeting us at the synagogue.

HIS

RABBI

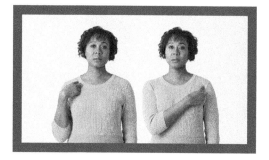

US

MEETING

WHERE?

SYNAGOGUE

RELATED VOCABULARY

BAR/BAT MITZVAH

PASSOVER

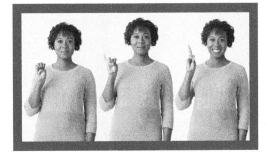

EID AL-FITR

LENT

EASTER

FULL: The non-dominant hand is in the S hand-shape, with the palm facing the side, and hand horizontal. The dominant hand is in the open B handshape. Slide the dominant hand across the top of the S handshape, out away from your body.

CELEBRATE: This is the same sign as ANNIVERSARY.

FEAST: Both hands are in the flat O handshape. In alternating arching movements, sign EAT without touching the hands to the mouth, but toward it.

GODSON: This is a combination of the signs GOD and SON.

BAPTIZE: Both of your hands are in the open A handshape, in the thumbs-up position. Dip your hands to your dominant side, laying them on their sides, and then bring them back up into the starting position.

RABBI: Place both R hands on your chest, near your collarbones. Your hands will naturally need to have your palms facing out so as not to hurt your wrists. Draw the hands down your chest. This is showing the robe the rabbi wears.

SYNAGOGUE: Your non-dominant hand is in the S handshape, with the palm facing down. Your domi-nant hand is also in the S handshape, with the palm facing out. Tap the base of your dominant hand on the back of your non-dominant hand twice. Another variation is to tap the first time with the S handshape and on the second tap your hand is in the Y handshape.

HIS/HER: Your dominant hand is the flat B handshape. Hold the hand out at a slight angle with the palm pointing toward the person you're referencing. If the person is not there, you point the palm to your side.

BAR/BAT MITZVAH: Both hands are in the S handshape, with the palms facing in. Hold the dominant hand over the non-dominant hand, and arms horizontal across the body. Circle the hands around each other, ending in the starting position.

PASSOVER: You sign PASSOVER the same as you sign CRACKER. Your non-dominant arm is bent with the hand near your dominant shoulder. Your dominant hand is in the A handshape and knocks on your elbow twice.

EID AL-FITR: Fingerspell E-I-D.

LENT: This is the sign for FASTING, but with your L handshape. Your dominant hand is in the L handshape. Place the thumb on the corner of your mouth, on the non-dominant side, and slide it across your lips, to end at the opposite corner of your mouth.

EASTER: Both hands are in the E handshape, hands held up near the chest, with palms staring out facing each other. Twist your hands forward two times so that the palms face out, then back in, and then back out.

GRAMMAR TIP: RHETORICAL QUESTIONS

You know there are two types of ASL questions: the WH-question and the yes/no question. There is another common type of question: the rhetorical question. You have seen this type of sentence throughout this workbook. In lesson 9.3, you'll see the sentence HIS RABBI US MEETING WHERE? SYNAGOGUE. The WHERE in the middle of the sentence is a rhetorical question in the sense that you (the signer) will answer it. It's a faster way to convey information.

You will see this used frequently with the WH-question sign WHY. You can think of this as a substitute for the word "because." SPRING I LIKE WHY? RAIN This would translate to "I like spring because of the rain." When you sign the WH-question sign in a rhetorical question, it's important that you raise your eyebrows as though asking a yes/no question rather than furrowing your eyebrows. You also hold the question sign for a brief moment before signing the remaining signs.

EXERCISE 9.3 FILL IN

Identify each sign. Write the answer in the space provided below each image.

1. ....

2. ....

3. ....

4. ....

5. ....

6. ....

7. ....

8. ....

CHAPTER 9 PROGRESS CHECK

Here are two phrases that use the vocabulary you've learned in chapter 9 and in some of the previous chapters. These are sentences you haven't seen yet. Identify the signs that make up each phrase. Write the answer in the spaces provided below each series of images. Once you're done, practice signing the complete sentences.

PHRASE 1

1. ....

2. ....

3. ....

4. ....

5. ....

PHRASE 2

6. ....

7. ....

8. ....

CONCLUSION

Congratulations on making your way through this workbook! Hopefully the images, practice exercises, and instruction have helped you gain a basic understanding of how to put signs together to build sentences in a simple and fun way. Maybe your family is on board with learning with you, too.

There are so many websites, apps, in-person courses, and community organizations to help you build on these skills so you'll continue to grow in ASL. I hope you'll use the resources listed on page 172 to continue making headway on your journey.

ANSWER KEY

Chapter 1

EXERCISE 1.1 FILL IN

1. N	7. R
2. L	8. X
3. A	9. E
4. I	10. G
5. Q	11. U
6. Y	12. C

EXERCISE 1.2 MULTIPLE CHOICE

1. B	4. B
2. A	5. A
3. C	6. C

EXERCISE 1.3 FILL IN

1. TOMORROW	5. MORNING
2. AFTERNOON	6. WHAT
3. TIME	7. YESTERDAY
4. APPOINTMENT	8. NIGHT

EXERCISE 1.4 WORD BANK

1. FEBRUARY	7. TODAY
2. DECEMBER	8. MONTH
3. YOU	9. YEAR
4. SATURDAY	10. SUNDAY
5. DAY	11. GO
6. MONDAY	

CHAPTER 1 PROGRESS CHECK

Phrase 1

1. TWO	4. I
2. THOUSAND	5. HAVE
3. DOLLAR	I have two thousand dollars.

Phrase 2

6. TOMORROW	9. GO
7. US-TWO	Tomorrow we'll go to lunch.
8. EAT-NOON	

Phrase 3

10. 10	14. HAVE
11. MORNING	I have an appointment at 10 in the morning.
12. I	
13. APPOINTMENT	

Phrase 4

15. TODAY	18. 15
16. WHAT	19. AUGUST
17. SATURDAY	Today is Saturday, August 15.

Chapter 2

EXERCISE 2.1 FILL IN

Phrase 1

1. HELLO
2. MY
3. NAME

Phrase 2

4. I
5. AGE
6. 27

Phrase 3

7. YOUR
8. NAME
9. WHAT

EXERCISE 2.2 MULTIPLE CHOICE

1. A
2. C
3. A
4. A

EXERCISE 2.3 FILL IN

1. HIKE
2. GAME
3. STORE
4. MOVIE
5. DANCE
6. WANT

EXERCISE 2.4 WORD BANK

1. PARTY
2. COME
3. ATTEND
4. INVITE
5. EMAIL
6. HOW MANY
7. FINISH
8. PEOPLE
9. ABLE

CHAPTER 2 PROGRESS CHECK

1. WINE
2. EMAIL
3. CHAT
4. START
5. NAME
6. PEOPLE
7. HELP
8. STORE
9. IMPROVE
10. WANT
11. DEAF
12. HELLO
13. TRY
14. LIVE
15. LEARN
16. COME

Chapter 3

EXERCISE 3.1 MULTIPLE CHOICE

1. B
2. A
3. C
4. B

EXERCISE 3.2 WORD BANK

1. GRANDPA
2. JAPAN
3. GRANDMA
4. RETIRE
5. SOON
6. COUSIN
7. MOVE
8. MOTHER-IN-LAW
9. LIVE
10. FATHER-IN-LAW

EXERCISE 3.3 FILL IN

1. BIRTHDAY
2. CELEBRATE
3. WEDDING
4. WEEKEND
5. SON
6. LAST WEEK
7. FUNERAL
8. RETIRE
9. GRADUATE
10. SISTER
11. ATTEND
12. RECENT

CHAPTER 3 PROGRESS CHECK

Phrase 1

1. LAST-WEEK
2. MY
3. GRANDMA
4. I
5. VISIT

I visited my grandma last week.

Phrase 2

6. TOMORROW
7. MY
8. MOM
9. FUNERAL
10. SHE
11. ATTEND

My mom's going to a funeral tomorrow.

Chapter 4

EXERCISE 4.1 WORD BANK

1. FRUSTRATED
2. UPSET
3. FEEL
4. ANGRY
5. SCARED
6. HAPPY
7. EXCITED
8. TRUE
9. SAD
10. WONDERFUL

EXERCISE 4.2 MULTIPLE CHOICE

1. A
2. A
3. B

EXERCISE 4.3 FILL IN

1. CUTE
2. AWESOME
3. DAUGHTER
4. ENJOY
5. SILLY
6. GOAL
7. FUNNY
8. SWEET

CHAPTER 4 PROGRESS CHECK

1. TERRIBLE
2. BOOK
3. SILLY
4. ENJOY
5. NERVOUS
6. CRY
7. STRESS
8. SWEET
9. AWESOME
10. HIMSELF (CAN ALSO BE HER-SELF OR ITSELF)
11. WORRY
12. EXCITED
13. WONDERFUL
14. INFLUENCE-ME
15. UPSET
16. ANGRY
17. FRUSTRATED
18. CONCERN
19. SAD
20. ME-HELP-YOU

Chapter 5

EXERCISE 5.1 FILL IN

1. DIABETES
2. MEDICINE
3. SICK
4. INFECTION
5. MYSELF
6. THROW-UP
7. TOOTH
8. HURT

EXERCISE 5.2 FILL IN

1. RIGHT
2. ALLERGIC
3. BREAK
4. NUT
5. WRONG
6. SOMETHING
7. FAST
8. GLUTEN FREE

EXERCISE 5.3 MULTIPLE CHOICE

1. B
2. A
3. B
4. A

EXERCISE 5.4 MULTIPLE CHOICE

1. C
2. B
3. C

CHAPTER 5 PROGRESS CHECK

Phrase 1

1. TOOTH
2. INFECTION
3. I
4. HAVE

I have a tooth infection.

Phrase 2

5. TOMORROW
6. MENSTRUATE
7. START
8. I

Tomorrow I'll start menstruating.

Chapter 6

EXERCISE 6.1 WORD BANK

1. JOB
2. MEETING
3. OFFICE
4. SECOND
5. WORK
6. PAYCHECK
7. DEPARTMENT
8. FLOOR

EXERCISE 6.2 MULTIPLE CHOICE

1. A
2. C
3. C
4. B

EXERCISE 6.3 FILL IN

1. COMPUTER
2. MOUSE
3. SYSTEM
4. COFFEE
5. PROGRAM

CHAPTER 6 PROGRESS CHECK

1. BOSS
2. WORK
3. COMPUTER
4. EMAIL
5. MEETING
6. EVENT
7. APPLY
8. PROGRAM
9. FUTURE

Chapter 7

EXERCISE 7.1 WORD BANK

1. TEXAS
2. ASIA
3. EUROPE
4. AUSTRALIA
5. NORTH AMERICA
6. NEW YORK
7. SOUTH AMERICA
8. CALIFORNIA
9. GROW-UP
10. AFRICA

EXERCISE 7.2 MULTIPLE CHOICE

1. A
2. C
3. B

EXERCISE 7.3 WORD BANK

1. COUNTRY
2. NORTH
3. LEFT
4. RIVER
5. CITY
6. SOUTH
7. RIGHT
8. WORLD
9. CONTINENTS
10. BIRD

CHAPTER 7 PROGRESS CHECK

1. RIVER
2. CITY
3. SEASON
4. SNOW
5. SUMMER
6. NORTH

Chapter 8

EXERCISE 8.1 FILL IN

1. ARRIVE
2. WHAT TIME
3. GET IN
4. LEAVE
5. HOW
6. RIDE IN

EXERCISE 8.2 MULTIPLE CHOICE

1. B
2. A
3. B
4. C

EXERCISE 8.3 WORD BANK

1. CANADA
2. HAWAII
3. HOTEL
4. RENTAL
5. WITH
6. ISLAND

CHAPTER 8 PROGRESS CHECK

1. C
2. A
3. A
4. B

Chapter 9

EXERCISE 9.1 MULTIPLE CHOICE

1. **B**
2. **A**
3. **C**
4. **C**
5. **B**

EXERCISE 9.2 WORD BANK

1. **HALLOWEEN**
2. **KISS-FIST**
3. **ST PATRICK'S DAY**
4. **THANKSGIVING**
5. **PARADE**
6. **WHAT-DO**
7. **VETERANS DAY**

EXERCISE 9.3 FILL IN

1. **EASTER**
2. **GOD SON**
3. **FULL**
4. **RABBI**
5. **CELEBRATE**
6. **BAPTIZE**
7. **FEAST**
8. **BAR/BAT MITZVAH**

CHAPTER 9 PROGRESS CHECK

Phrase 1

1. **YOUR**
2. **FAMILY**
3. **CELEBRATE**
4. **EID**
5. **HOW**

   How does your family celebrate Eid al-Fitr?

Phrase 2

6. **LAST-WEEK**
7. **ST PATRICK'S DAY**
8. **WHAT-DO**

   What did you do for St Patrick's Day last week?

RESOURCES

Sites for Learning ASL

ASL Rochelle: aslrochelle.com

Dawn Sign Press: dawnsign.com

Gallaudet University: gallaudet.edu/asl-connect

Life Print University: lifeprint.com

National Association of the Deaf: nad.org

Apps

The ASL App

ASL Dictionary

ASL Dictionary from NTID

ASL for the Classroom

Marlee Signs

Engage Your Community

ASL Slam: Aslslam.com

Deaf Expos

Deaf Linx: deaflinx.com

Your local RID chapter

Google Search for a Deaf coffee chat, Deaf club, or ASL club in your city

Your local college or university may have an ASL Club and will know of more resources for learning and practice in the Deaf community around you

REFERENCES

Bar-Tzur, David. The Interpreter's
Friend. Accessed November 2019.
theinterpretersfriend.org.

Global Deaf Muslim. "Purpose of Ramadan."
Posted August 9, 2013. YouTube
video, 4:53. YouTube.com/watch?v
=jXHgZxuCyHk&list=PLZMLUr11wecNh3
__VPXdjHQKkXkGxZqRi&index=4

No Barriers Zen Temple. "ASL Sign for
'Temple.'" Posted July 14, 2017. YouTube video,
0:08. YouTube.com/watch?v=rKxhrxVO8YU.

INDEX

ACKNOWLEDGMENTS

I'd like to thank my ASL students for their eagerness and excitement for learning and communicating with sign language. Their determination to communicate with everyone they meet is inspiring. Their deep love for others and ASL is an invigorating daily reminder of the impact that one person has on another. I thank each of them for making teaching ASL fun and rewarding.

I'm grateful to Nick and my children for their excitement and support. I'm grateful to my editor, Erin Nelson, for her vision and guidance.

ABOUT THE AUTHOR

Rochelle Barlow first began to learn ASL as a young child. She studied and practiced on her own for many years and then with private tutors, in high school classes, and as a Deaf Education student at Utah State University. She worked at the School for the Deaf and Blind in Ogden, Utah, and interpreted after college for many higher education institutions. Rochelle began teaching ASL to families and individuals over fifteen years ago, expanding her instruction to local community centers, co-ops, and private schools and classrooms. She then launched her own business, teaching ASL online at "ASL Rochelle." Rochelle loves to read, write, belt out music from the '20s to the '60s, and watch British murder mysteries. She is the mother of six incredible children and lives in southern Oregon.

Printed in the USA
CPSIA information can be obtained
at www.ICGtesting.com
LVHW050047101223
765801LV00005B/34